THE
BABY BOOM

3-12-22

P. J. O'ROURKE

THE BABY BOOM

*How It Got That Way
And It Wasn't My Fault
And I'll Never Do It Again*

Grove Press UK

First published in the United States in 2014 by Atlantic Monthly Press, an imprint of Grove/Atlantic, Inc.

Published in hardback in Great Britain in 2014 by Grove Press UK, an imprint of Grove/Atlantic, Inc.

This paperback edition published in Great Britian in 2015 by Grove Press UK

10 9 8 7 6 5 4 3 2 1

A CIP catalogue record for this book is available from the British Library.

Paperback ISBN: 978 1 61185 558 6
E-book ISBN: 978 1 61185 979 9

Printed and bound by CPI Group (UK) Ltd, Croydon, CR0 4YY

Grove Press, UK
An Imprint of Grove/Atlantic Inc.
Ormond House
26–27 Boswell Street
London
WC1N 3JZ

www.groveatlantic.com

The Baby Boom is dedicated to the memory of
Clifford Bronson O'Rourke and Delphine Loy O'Rourke,
progenitors thereof.

Thou shalt not answer questionnaires
Or quizzes upon World-Affairs,
  Nor with compliance
Take any test. Thou shalt not sit
With statisticians nor commit
  A social science.
     —W. H. Auden
     from "Under Which Lyre"

CONTENTS

In lapidary inscriptions a man is not upon oath.
—Dr. Samuel Johnson

PREFACE TO A BOOK ATTEMPTING TO CAPTURE THE SPIRIT OF A GENERATION OF GOD'S FAVORITE SPOILED BRATS

Herein is a ballad of the Baby Boom, not a dissertation on it. A rhapsody, not a report. A freehand sketch, not a faithful rendering. That is to say, I am—it is a writer's vocation and the métier of his age cohort—full of crap.

Characters, the narrator included, have been drawn from nature and not from individuals. Essence has been added and *accidens* has been omitted. Merry hell has been played with time, place, personages, and recalled dialogue. Twice-told tales have been trotted out onto the court for three-peats. (And, come now, fellow Baby Boomers, confess your own guilt to the same.) Only the most outrageous and unbelievable things in this book are recounted exactly as they happened.

UK INTRODUCTION

It is with no little trepidation that I dish out this slumgullion of Americana to British readers. Post-war experience in America was very different from post-war experience in a place where war, in fact, occurred. That is, we had the "post-" and you had the war.

There were "Baby Booms" in both nations. (Don't look at me if yours started a little early due to GIs being "overpaid, over-sexed and over here." My dad was in the Pacific.)

America's Baby Boom got the benefit of a period of social stability and strong economic growth. Britain's Baby Boom got the benefit of Obamacare, before computer access to universal health service had been perfected the way it has been by the current American president.

Your food and clothing remained rationed until the early 1950s. We plumped up and dressed in silly coonskin caps.

You disposed of your old empire. (I've been to many former British overseas possessions and don't know why you wanted them in the first place, but the world map did look nicer with all that pink.) We went looking for a new one—in all the wrong places such as up along the Yalu River and on the underside of Chiang Kai-shek and in South Vietnam.

And the American car culture was an important factor in the lives of our Baby Boom. Meanwhile the British car culture was . . .

Mind you I'm a fan of British cars, having owned a number of them including a 1960 MGA, the wooden floorboards of which gave way leaving the heels of my shoes grinding the pavement at 40 mph. Also the electrical components manufactured by Lucas (company motto: "Home By Dark") would periodically catch fire.

Let's just say the British car culture was different.

Of course, in many ways, Britain was far ahead of the United States. All we were able to produce was common, garden-variety juvenile delinquents. You were cultivating rare and exquisite breeds: Teddy Boys, Rockers, Mods. For all I know the Droogs in Anthony Burgess' *A Clockwork Orange* are pictures drawn from life.

Your Skiffle bands, horrid as they were, represented a vast improvement on the folk musicians who gave America's Baby Boom its first taste of "alternative" music. From those Skiffle bands came a few musicians who would greatly influence the Baby Boom on both sides of the Atlantic and who were, to be honest, not bad. John Lennon for instance. Although he was, of course, no Otis Redding.

And the BBC's 1950s children's television programming was worse by miles than what we had in America. Bad television for young people is extremely important to their growth and development. It promotes going outside and getting exercise and fresh air. It establishes a healthy skepticism about the wisdom and intelligence of people in authority. And it teaches the important lesson that adults who pretend to be very, very fond of children are...

Somehow I feel that I'm not making the best sales pitch for my book. And Americans are supposed to be so good at selling things. Invasion of Iraq, for example.

There's probably no good reason for anyone who isn't American to read about the American Baby Boom. Except America's Baby Boomers are all over the world poking our noses—and our drones—into everything. (Three U.S. presidents from this generation and, with Hillary Clinton, still counting . . .) So I suppose understanding us is useful in a don't-smoke-while-dousing-the-effigy-with-petrol-on-Guy-Fawkes-Night way.

Let me start over with a personal plea. I read every word of *Fever Pitch* by Nick Hornby (fellow Baby Boomer, though one of your lot). I hadn't the slightest what Hornby was on about. I gather the subject was a game he mistakenly called "football." (Interesting that we pay our hooligans a salary and put them on the field while yours seem to operate on a volunteer basis.) And I enjoyed the book immensely.

But now I've put a foot wrong again, as if I'm comparing myself to Nick Hornby, which would be like comparing Posh Spice's career as a midfielder to David Beckham's. And even my apology is bollocks since Beckham never played for Arsenal. What I'm trying to say is that we are all members of a single vast and splendid worldwide English-speaking culture. (Well, the Americans can *speak* English, more or less, while the British can read and write it as well, but you know what I mean.) As fellow members of that vast and splendid culture we should support each other's cultural endeavors, which, in this case, means you ought to buy my book although you'll haven't the slightest what I'm on about.

> P. J. O'Rourke
> March Hare Farm
> New Hampshire
> Candlemass (or, as we call it in the States, Super Bowl Sunday), 2014

There was a generation,
    That had a lot of hair,
Right in the middle of their forehead.
    When they were good,
    They were very good indeed,
But when they were bad they were horrid.
        —with apologies to Henry Wadsworth Longfellow

PROLOGUE

We Are the World

We are the generation that changed everything. Of all the eras and epochs of Americans, ours is the one that made the biggest impression—on ourselves. But that's an important accomplishment because we're the generation that created the self, made the firmament of the self, divided the light of the self from the darkness of the self, and said let there be self. If you were born between 1946 and 1964, you may have noticed this *your*self.

That's not to say we're a selfish generation. Selfish means "too concerned with the self," and we're not. Self isn't something we're just, you know, concerned with. We *are* self.

Before us, self was without form and void, like our parents in their dumpy clothes and vague ideas. Then we came along. Now the personal is the political. The personal is the socioeconomic. The personal is the religious and the secular, science and the arts. The personal is every thing that creepeth upon the earth after his (and, let us hasten to add, her) kind. If the Baby Boom has done one thing it's to beget a personal universe.

And our apologies to anyone who personally happens to be a jerk. Self is like fish, proverbially speaking. Give a man a fish and you've fed him for a day. Teach a man to fish and, if he turns into a dry-fly catch-and-release angling fanatic up to his liver in icy water wearing ridiculous waders and an absurd hat, pestering trout with three-pound test line on a thousand-dollar graphite rod, and going on endlessly about Royal Coachman lures that he tied himself using muskrat fur and partridge feathers . . . well, at least his life partner is glad to have him out of the house.

We made the universe personal, and we made the universe new. New in the sense of juvenescent. We have an abiding admiration for our own larval state.

We saw that the grown-ups were like primitive insects. They never underwent metamorphosis. They didn't emerge from their home and office cocoons with brilliant, fluttering wings. They just continued to molt, getting more gross, lumpy, and bald and, as it were, bugging us. Better that we should stay nymphs and naiads. Plus we were having more fun than the adults of the species.

"Don't ever change!" we wrote in each other's high school yearbooks. "Stay just the way you are!" What strange valedictions to give ourselves on the threshold of life. Imagine if we had obeyed them, and now everyone possessed the resolute solipsism of adolescence with its wild enthusiasms, dark lethargies, strong lusts, keen aversions, inner turmoils, and uncontained impulses. Life would be exactly like it is today. You're welcome.

So here we are in the Baby Boom cosmos, formed in our image, personally tailored to our individual needs, and predetermined to be eternally fresh and novel. And we saw that it was good. Or pretty good.

We should have had a cooler name, the way the Lost Generation did. Except good luck to anybody who tries to tell us to get lost. Anyway it's too late now, we're stuck with being forever described as exploding infants. And maybe it's time, now that we've splattered ourselves all over the place, for the Baby Boom to look back and think. "What made us who we are?" "And what caused us to act the way we do?" "And WTF?" Because the truth is, if we hadn't decided to be young forever, we'd be old.

The youngest Baby Boomers, born in the last year when anybody thought it was hip to like Lyndon Johnson, are turning fifty. Those of us who were born when postwar birthrates were highest, even before Ike was liked, won't (statistics tell us) have to wait as long for death as we had to wait to get laid.

We'd be sad about this if we weren't too busy remarrying younger wives, reviving careers that hit glass ceilings when children arrived, and renewing prescriptions for drugs that keep us from being sad. And we'll never retire. We can't. The mortgage is underwater. We're in debt up to the Rogaine for the kids' college education. And it serves us right—we're the generation who insisted that a passion for living should replace working for one.

Nonetheless it's an appropriate moment for us to weigh what we've wrought and tally what we've added to and subtracted from existence. We've reached the age of accountability. The world is our fault. We are the generation that has an excuse for everything—one of our greatest contributions to modern life—but the world is still our fault. This is every generation's fate. It's a matter of power and privilege demography. Whenever anything happens anywhere, somebody over fifty signs the bill for it. And the Baby Boom, seated as we are at the head of life's table, is hearing Generation X, Generation Y, and the Millennials all saying, "Check, please!"

How can he get wisdom . . . whose talk is of bullocks?
—Ecclesiasticus 38:25,
The Apocrypha

1

A REGULAR OLD
BABY BOOMER SPEAKS

To address America's Baby Boom is to face big, broad problems. We number more than 75 million, and we're not only diverse but take a thorny pride in our every deviation from the norm (even though we're in therapy for it). We are all alike about us each being unusual.

Fortunately we are all alike about big, broad problems too. We won't face them. There's a website for that, a support group to join, a class to take, alternative medicine, regular exercise, a book that explains it all, a celebrity on TV who's been through the same thing, or we can eliminate gluten from our diet. History is full of generations that had too many problems. We are the first generation to have too many answers.

Not a problem. Consider the people who have faced up squarely to the deepest and most perplexing conundrums of existence. Leo Tolstoy, for example. He tackled every one of them. Why are we here? What kind of life should we lead? The nature of evil. The character of love. The essence of identity. Salvation. Suffering. Death.

What did it get him? Dead, for one thing. And off his rocker for the last thirty years of his life. Plus he was saddled with a thousand-page novel about war, peace, and everything else you can think of, which he couldn't even look up on Wikipedia to get the skinny on because he hadn't written it yet. What a life. If Leo Tolstoy had been one of us he could have entered a triathlon, a Baby Boom innovation of the middle 1970s. By then we knew we couldn't run away from our problems. *But* if we added cycling and swimming . . .

So to the problems of talking about the Baby Boom let us turn our big, broad (yet soon to be firmed up due to the triathlon for seniors that we're planning to enter) generational backsides.

Nonetheless, a difficulty remains. Most groups of people who get tagged by history as a "generation" can be described in an easy, offhand way: folks sort of the same age experiencing sort of the same things in sort of the same place, like the cast of *Cheers* or *Seinfeld* or *Friends*. I'm almost sure—as a result of taking Modern Literature in college—that Ernest Hemingway, F. Scott and Zelda Fitzgerald, James Joyce, Gertrude Stein, Ford Madox Ford, Henry Miller, and Ezra Pound were roommates in a big apartment on the Left Bank in Paris in the 1920s. (If not, I give the sitcom idea free to the reader.)

But the Baby Boom has an exact definition, a precise demography. We are the children who were born during a period after World War II when the long-term trend in fertility among American women was exceeded. Our mothers began this excess abruptly in 1946. They peaked in their use of the stuff that makes babies in 1947, and thereafter they gradually tapered off until in 1964 they were taking the pill or rolling over and pretending to be asleep or telling their husbands, "Go phone the pope about where to buy rubbers."

As a generation, we are spread across the huge space of America and span so much time that the oldest Baby Boomers are sometimes the parents—usually via an oopsie—of the youngest Baby Boomers. (It's painful to think how many of those babies were put up for adoption because it was too soon for the Baby Boom to have soothed the fierce mores of society. Shame was still felt about "illegitimate" children as if the cooings, gurgles, and spit-ups of some infants conformed to established rules and regulations while the cooings, gurgles, and spit-ups of other infants weren't legal. On the other hand, in fairness, society may have had an inkling of just how hard it would be to extract child support payments from Baby Boom fathers.)

Anyway, distinctions among varieties of Baby Boomers need to be made. Geographical distinctions are peripatetically moot for us. I have a friend who says he got so stoned in the 1960s that the next thing he remembers is standing in line for a Procol Harem concert at New York's Fillmore East with a ticket in his hand for a Procol Harem concert at San Francisco's Fillmore West. Distinctions according to race, class, gender, or sexual orientation would be offensive to Baby Boom sensitivities. Furthermore they'd be beside the point because the author—much as he endeavors to be as different from everyone else as a member of the Baby Boom should be—finds himself to be hopelessly ordinary in matters of race, class, gender identification, and which section of *Playboy* he turned to first when he was sixteen.

But time is a distinction we all have to endure. And there are temporal variations in the Baby Boom. We have our seniors, our juniors, our sophomores, and our freshman.

The seniors were born in the late 1940s. The author is of that ilk. This book is necessarily written from the ilk's point of view. The first pronouncement of the Baby Boom is "I have to be me." It's as if we think the pronouncements of all those who came before us were something like, "I have to be Gerald and Betty Ford." Then Dad's hair began to thin and he whacked somebody with a golf ball and Mom got a little tipsy. The Baby Boom speaks the truth.

The seniors were on the bow wave of the Baby Boom's voyage of exploration. But they were also closely tethered in the wake of preceding generations. In effect the seniors were keelhauled by the Baby Boom experience and left a bit soggy and shaken. If we wound up as financial advisers trying to wear tongue studs or Trotskyites trying to organize Tea Party protests, or both, we are to be forgiven. Hillary Clinton and Cheech Marin are seniors.

The juniors were born in the early 1950s. They were often younger siblings of the seniors and came of age when parents were throwing in the towel during the "What's the Matter with Kids These Days" feature match. The juniors pursued the notions, whims, and fancies of the Baby Boom with a greater intensity. For them drugs were no longer experimental; drugs were proven. John Belushi was technically a senior, born in 1949, but, knowing John, he was probably held back a couple of grades and can be counted as a junior. From the juniors we get the teeny-boppers, the groupies, and the more ragamuffin barefoot urchins of Haight-Ashbury. They hunted up some shoes when they eventually made their way to Silicon Valley. (Bill Gates and Steve Jobs were both born in 1955.) But they never did find their neckties.

The sophomores were born in the late 1950s. By the time they reached adolescence the Baby Boom ethos had permeated society. Sophomores gladly accepted sex, drugs, rock and roll, and the deep philosophical underpinning thereof. But they'd seen enough of the Baby Boom in action to realize that what works in general terms doesn't always work when the bong sets fire to the beanbag chair. Circumstances had changed. In college many of the sophomores attended classes. Some even snuck off and got MBAs. I have a friend who went to Stanford in 1973. The Stanford campus is home to the redoubtable conservative Hoover Institution think tank. When my friend arrived at the school the Hoover Institution's office windows were boarded up as high as a rock could be thrown. (We're not the most athletic generation, so the windows didn't have to be boarded up too far.) That year the boards were taken down. The sophomores were the authors of *The Official Preppy Handbook*.

The freshmen were born in the early 1960s. All that the Baby Boom had wrought was, for them, a given. What we accomplished with blood, sweat, and tears or, really, with buds, sweat, other lubricants, and tear gas or, in actual fact, with listening to Blood, Sweat & Tears, especially "Spinning Wheel," over and over again on the record player while we stared at the amazing kaleidoscopic patterns in the linoleum, freshmen took for granted.

They felt no visceral effects from the events that formed the Baby Boom. To freshmen the Vietnam War was just something that was inexplicably on TV all the time like Ed McMahon. Feminism had gone from a pressing social issue to a Bea Arthur comedy show that their parents liked, and, by the time the freshmen were in college, feminism was an essay topic for the "Reading Shakespeare in Cultural Context" course. Hint: Lady Macbeth hit that glass ceiling hard.

Freshmen have no personal memory of the Kennedy and King assassinations, which showed the tragedy inherent in greatness and taught the Baby Boom to stop just short of it, the way Bill Clinton did. They may have suffered a momentary golden oldies pang when John Lennon was shot, thinking, maybe, "Now the original Wings will never be reunited."

The freshmen didn't witness the monumental civil rights movement. They were taught that it was monumental in school. Being taught that a thing is monumental in school turns it into an intellectually unvisited memorial, a Grant's Tomb of the mind. To the freshmen racism, sexism, and homophobia are as much slurs as facts. They don't even stop to puzzle over the evil the way I stopped at an Alabama gas station on a 1959 car trip to Florida to puzzle over the drinking fountain labeled "colored." Not that I was puzzling over evil at the moment, because I had no idea what "colored" could have to do with a drinking fountain. Colored water? Bad idea. Why would anybody want it?

And that's pretty much as far as freshmen get with moral reasoning about America. Good for them. They live in a better country. They have the luxury of fretting over things like the deficit, the one-percenters, the congressional deadlock, the fairness of the nation's health insurance system, and whether, if they spend a lot of time at the gym and get a tattoo, they stand any chance of hooking up with twenty-six-year-olds.

They're still Baby Boomers. The freshmen may be different in many ways from the Baby Boom's upper classmen, but there's no mistaking them for members of any of the younger and duller (if hotter) generations.

The tip-off is the blather, the jabber, the prattle, the natter, the gab, gas, yak, yap, baloney, blarney, bunkum, the jaw-slinging, tongue-wagging, gum-beating chin music that is the Baby Boom's gift to the world. Stephen Colbert is a freshman. So is Ann Coulter. So are Jon Stewart, Sarah Palin, Conan O'Brien, and Larry the Cable Guy.

Among prominent freshmen Baby Boomers is President Barack Obama. There was a controversy when he was running for president that showed how much of a freshman Baby Boomer President Obama is and also illustrated what an extraordinary change the Baby Boom has made in the nature of American flapdoodle.

President and Mrs. Obama were members of Trinity United Church of Christ in Chicago. Trinity's pastor until early 2008 was the Reverend Jeremiah Wright. Reverend Wright had married Mr. and Mrs. Obama and baptized their children. Reverend Wright is a man of strong views, forcefully delivered, and, shall we say, not always tactfully put.

In a sermon after 9/11 Reverend Wright said, "We bombed Hiroshima, we bombed Nagasaki, and we nuked far more than the thousands in New York and the Pentagon, and we never batted an eye . . . and now we are indignant because the stuff we have done overseas is now brought back into our own front yard." In another sermon he said, "The government lied about inventing the HIV virus as a means of genocide against people of color." And, most famously, he said, "God damn America."

Now, a senior Baby Boomer, especially in the senior Baby Boom's 1960s heyday, would have been standing on a pew, clenched fist raised in the air, shouting in response with fervid suggestions for righteous action probably involving property damage at the nearby University of Chicago. A sophomore Baby Boomer, assuming the sophomore was awake early enough for a church service and could find the church, would have been nodding in stoned agreement and hoping that Trinity United's activist social ministry included free lunch. A junior Baby Boomer would have been muttering to himself, "That might be pitching things a bit high and inside." But a freshman Baby Boomer . . .

The controversy played out after various news organizations and political opponents took professional umbrage at Reverend Wright's sermons with anticlimatic results. Although Senator Obama sat in the congregation, there was no indication that he paid any attention whatsoever to Reverend Wright.

The freshman Baby Boomer was born into a sea of hooey and swims about comfortably therein unaware that other environments of discourse exist. For all we know, while the Reverend Jeremiah Wright fulminated and swore, the future president was fiddling with his BlackBerry blabbing to Rahm Emanuel. It is the Baby Boom way.

Once people spoke their minds. And what awful things we heard (cf. Rev. Wright—born 1941—above). Baby Boom speech is not mindless but there's a cardiac bypass. We speak from the heart and that's not the half of it. We speak from the gut, from the spleen, from the liver's bile ducts, out our butts, through our hats; even our T-shirts cannot shut up with the things we have to say, never mind social media and talk-radio talk-show call-in callers. We talk until the cows come home, and who keeps cows anymore. We talk of cabbages and kings, as well we might, because who among us can tell the king of Saudi Arabia from a cabbage, burnoose aside. We found drugs—speed, cocaine, Starbucks—that were talk itself in pill, powder, and custom frappuccino form.

And yet one thing that cannot be said about the Baby Boom is "It's all talk." You can't say that about a generation whose powers of language are so fundamentally transformative that one of its members ran for president using the name "Barack" when everybody knows he's called Barry.

America in the two decades after World War II was full to the point of sloshing over with motive, means, and opportunity. There was a feeling that children born into this age of high purpose, wide prosperity, and handsome prospects could be or do anything. It wasn't a fact. But facts are faint things next to feelings. Facts are acknowledged, feelings are *felt*.

What makes the Baby Boom different from other generations is the way everybody was feeling we could be or do anything. What unifies the Baby Boom is the way we talked everybody into letting us get away with it.

We know nothing of to-morrow; our business is to be good and happy to-day.

—Reverend Sydney Smith

2

A GOOD AND HAPPY PLACE

Personally speaking (and personally is the only way our generation does speak and personally is the only way a book about the Baby Boom could be written), I think the world we've changed should be measured against the world as it was when the Baby Boom was a baby. There was a life we got before we got life by the throat. And personally speaking—in an average kind of family in an average sort of neighborhood in an average part of America—this was a pleasant life, on average.

Among the earliest memories I can summon is one of pure awe, the kind produced by our first glimpse of the Rockies or of enormous surf or, to use a more apt comparison, of anything on the screen when we got our first television. And I do mean anything. *Farm Report. Mass for Shut-ins. The Today Show* with Dave Garroway, coanchored by a chimpanzee named J. Fred Muggs. (Not as attractive as Katie Couric but as incisive.)

However, we didn't get a television until the average—50 percent by 1953—American household did. So I'm standing at a living room window, chin on the sill, watching the big kids walk to school.

All children, at all times, have wanted to be adults, except the Baby Boom. We wanted to be older, greater children. There were plenty of them going by my house. Every neighborhood had lots of kids in those days, though "the baby boom" was hardly under way. Come to think of it, every neighborhood had lots of parents. There was a daily parade of generations to be viewed.

I was looking at the march of the Silent Generation. Not that they were silent coming down the sidewalks. They were, I noted with envy, making the glorious racket of free individuals out and about on their own. They seemed, as well as I was able to form such a thought, to be the very personification of riotous autonomy. They did invent rock and roll, after all. Some of them built loud hotrods. Some indulged in clamorous behavior that had the nation fretting about juvenile delinquency.

The Baby Boom would have an ultimately disappointing relationship with the Silent Generation. Sometimes the relationship started with older siblings, more often with the babysitter. My babysitter would play rock and roll on our phonograph, and a boy with a ducktail haircut would visit her when the grown-ups were safely gone. Bill Haley and His Comets didn't sound like much to a child's ears, thumpy and repetitive, but the music had a kind of disturbed urgency. Children like disturbance. I urgently hoped the babysitter and the boy with a ducktail haircut would do something disturbing, like let me look at the switchblade knife that boys with ducktail haircuts were said to carry or play doctor with each other. (Maybe that happened on the couch after I'd been put to bed, but the generation that was born too late for service in World War II was also born too early for much beyond a dry hump.) As far as I could tell, the most transgressive thing they did was make popcorn without permission.

The Silent Generation seemed to hold an unfulfilled promise of interesting social agitation. The term "Silent Generation" was coined in a 1951 cover article from *Time* magazine, then as now the digest of what educated cement heads think. *Time* wrote, "Youth today is waiting for the hand of fate to fall on its shoulders [the Korean War wasn't fate enough?], meanwhile working fairly hard and saying almost nothing."

Mort Sahl, Dick Gregory, George Carlin, Richard Pryor, and everyone in Monty Python were members of the Silent Generation. Although it turns out they were just kidding. The hand of fate appeared to be always almost ready to fall upon the shoulders of the Silent Generation and turn them into James Dean or Maynard G. Krebs. But they couldn't quite get the goatee to grow or find a Porsche to crash.

Speaking of fate and its hands, there's never been a Silent Generation president, unless we count Jimmy Carter, who was technically a member of the Greatest Generation but didn't graduate from the Naval Academy until 1946. This generational chief executive lacuna is probably the result of what students of the electoral process call "the road trip factor." Going on a road trip with a Baby Boomer president would be bad enough. Barack Obama having smug disagreements with the GPS, telling it, "This is a debate I want to have." Bill Clinton driving off the road every time a pedestrian with breasts appeared. George H. W. Bush might have been fun once, before he gave up beer. But think about going on a road trip with Jimmy Carter.

Somehow the Silent Generation was mostly just noise. They are the generation who ultimately surrendered to adulthood. We are the generation who kept fighting the battles of adolescence down to the present day. Between the Baby Boom and the Silent Generation there is a marked difference in outlook, opinion, and polyester Sansabelt pants.

My other glowing toddler memory is Dad coming home from work. The Greatest Generation arrives. The sight of my father driving up the driveway produces an exultant thrill. And not just because he often brought a toy.

We in the Baby Boom had an unadulterated love for our parents that few children, past or future, have matched. Maybe we surpassed what other children felt for their parents because, in the past, children grew up in colder and more crowded homes with mushier meals and the razor strap still hanging by the bathroom sink, and, in the future, children had us for moms and dads.

Our parents didn't get divorced. They didn't hit us much. If they were neurotic they had the good manners to have a drink instead of a long talk with us about it. They were stricter (or are remembered as being so) than we would be with our kids. But they were less pestering and intrusive. A Greatest Generation parent was as likely to turn up at school blaming a teacher for his kid's poor arithmetic grade as Xi

Jinping is likely to turn up at Amnesty International blaming Bono for his country's poor human rights record. Our parents may have been distant by modern standards, but a certain distance is helpful in adulation.

I remember riding in the car with my mother, lolling around on the front seat as children were allowed to do. I looked at her face, sunlit in profile, and was so stricken by her beauty and so overwhelmed by my love for her that I despaired of any adequate positive expression of my feelings and reached over and pulled the hood release on the Buick.

And only a few years later we would hold this generation in categorical contempt. During the 1960s we would talk about our parents, as a group, in a way that today we would be embarrassed to talk about militant Islamic fundamentalists, as a group. Our depth and breadth of prejudice would shock every one of our twenty-first-century sensibilities, if we ever thought about it. Which we don't because, later still, we got all soppy and sentimental about the Greatest Generation just in time to put them in nursing homes or the grave.

In my fledgling recollections, the Jazz Age generation is also somewhere around the house. Every neighborhood had lots of grandparents, too, although their exact function wasn't clear. They weren't leading their own lives the way grandparents do today. Nor were they raising the kids their kids had abandoned to their care. They certainly weren't having second careers. A job did not define a person in the Jazz Age. Jay Gatsby didn't even have a job. One career, at the very most, used to be considered enough.

Grandma's 1920s had had flaming youth, rude manners, shocking fashions, permissive sex, illegal drugs in the bathtub gin, atrocious music, and sillier dancing than a Grateful Dead concert's. Everything the Baby Boom set out to do in the 1960s had been done already, forty years before. But, suddenly and completely, it had disappeared.

Our beliefs and behaviors would live on. After another forty years (and counting) we can tune in NPR, turn on MSNBC, or drop out on the couch with the Sunday *New York Times* and be reimmersed in our groovy notions of yore. We can visit Burning Man, an Occupy Whatnot demonstration, or Portland, Oregon, and see our bygone selves replicated with a few additional piercings and neck tattoos.

If we weren't so used to this it would be astonishing—as though we'd arrived on campus in 1967 to find all the coeds in cloche hats with stockings rolled down to their knees and "Oh You Kid" written in grease pencil on their yellow rain slickers, singing "Yes! We Have No Bananas" and voicing strong opinions on the pressing question of whether girls should bob their hair.

Were the twenties a failed experiment at having a sixties, like a first attempt at a space launch blowing up on the pad? Or do anomalies in youthful *Weltanschauung* pop up from time to time in a meaningless fashion? There've been such blips in the past—the Romantic movement, the French Revolution. But they didn't have a generation like the Baby Boom to make it stick.

Still, it is a mystery how the flappers and whoopee makers and bright young things wound up as our grandparents, wearing aprons over ugly, flowered housedresses or baggy pants mismatched to old suit coats, puttering in the garden, muttering to themselves in the kitchen, and looking out over the tops of their bifocals puzzled at our 1950s childhood world, which was, one would think, so much less puzzling than the hip flask and 23 skidoo world that had been theirs.

Actually, my own grandmother would have been the wrong person to ask about these things. Presbyterian daughter of a downstate county sheriff and widow of a postmaster appointed by Calvin Coolidge, she was the kind of Republican who was still mad at Roosevelt—*Teddy* Roosevelt, for splitting the Republican Party in 1912 and allowing a Woodrow Wilson to be elected. (There are hazards in generational generalizations.) But I had another elderly relative. As far as I knew he was a retired supermarket meat cutter whose main interest was pitching horseshoes. One time in my twenties I deigned to sit and talk with him—it was Christmas or something. He had played trumpet in the band at a speakeasy with a whorehouse upstairs.

Numerous mysteries would unfold and were unfolding in the quotidian existence of the 1950s. The idea that we had an uncomplicated and sterile past is an invention to flatter ourselves about our complex and richly organic present.

There was the mystery of what was in the attic. Something large and horrible, I was sure. The door to the attic stairs opened into my room. I couldn't go to sleep until I'd checked two or three times to make sure that the hook and eye latch was fastened. I don't recall considering what kind of large and horrible thing would be stopped by a small hook and eye in a cheap hollow door. Anyway, there was something worse in the basement. To be sent down there after dark to get a clean pair of socks for school the next day was to experience fear beyond telling. And the night wind gave dreadful clawing shapes to the branches on the tree in the front yard.

Never mind that the house had been built the year before. The tree still had the fabric from the plant nursery wrapped around its trunk and was under four feet tall. The basement was brightly lit, as yet uncluttered, and so clean and dry that I could smell the concrete curing in the foundation. And the cobweb-free attic barely had room for the two suitcases and one broken cane chair it contained. We are an imaginative generation.

Our parents weren't. Or, rather, they deliberately chose not to be. Our parents put a lot of thought and planning into the avoidance of imagination. This is the solution to the mystery of the houses we grew up in, which were too ugly to have been designed and decorated simply by accident.

Every imaginable disaster seemed to have occurred in our parents' lifetime—financial panic, sudden spread of grinding poverty, absurd popular ideologies, fanatical governments, systematic murder of millions of innocents, military conflict everywhere in the world, and the invention of a bomb that would obliterate a whole city. For any further imagination, our parents had no use.

The exception was their cars. With automobiles the Greatest Generation let imagination take flight, almost literally, given the aviational sheet metal on some of their vehicles. The cars of the 1950s and '60s are a byword, almost a synonym, for crass materialistic excess. Intellectuals, to this day, lodge particular complaint against the tail fins. Perhaps they take the ornamental use of fins personally, many intellectuals being fishy types. But upswept rear fenders and the equally inveighed against lavish application of chrome are the least of what make the era's American cars astounding.

Some are strange, such as the 1950 "bathtub" Hudson and the which-way-did-it-go 1950 Studebaker. Some are stranger, like the 1960 Plymouth Valiant, which looks as if its styling was done by four men who lacked a common language working together in a dark room.

Some are examples of industrial design perfected, with form following function and function chasing a beauty all its own—the 1953 through 1955 Studebakers and the Willys Jeep Station Wagon that stayed in production, almost without visible changes, from 1946 to 1965.

Some are works of art. You can tell by the way Baby Boomers, paying through the nose, fill our garages with these instead of with Rothkos. There's the 1948 Chrysler Town and Country convertible, the 1955 Ford Thunderbird, the 1955 Chevrolet Nomad, the 1965 Ford Mustang, and all Corvettes until 1973 when they start to get too trial-separation-and-combover-looking.

And some of the Greatest Generation's cars are an amazement. For example, the 1959 Chevrolet Biscayne. Here was Chevy's least expensive model, a get-to-worker, mommy-shopper, kiddie-hauler budget conveyance. And—hydra headlamps, dagger-slit hood scoops, gridiron grill big enough for a cannibal roast with seven chrome nipples down the fifty-yard line, tail lights like the giant fangs of a basilisk, and two great hatchet-edged swoops of steel across the trunk lid—it makes the Batmobile look like a Scion xB.

I have digressed here, I know, like any good Baby Boom boy my age would. Give us a look at four square feet of the bodywork on any car built between World War II and the Arab oil embargo and we'll tell you the make, model, and year with more accuracy than we get from our PSA tests. But it is worth noting that the Greatest Generation took all of its creativity, artistic feeling, and aesthetic sensibilities and put them on wheels. It's as if they felt, "Okay, okay, we *do* have an imagination, but let's make sure we can *get it out of here!*"

Their cars aside, the postwar life the Greatest Generation wanted for themselves and for us was a unique combination of the intensely dynamic and the adamantly prosaic. And this is the life they got. It was fantasy-free fantasy fulfillment and science fiction, hold the fiction.

Hence my house, built in 1951. It was not a pseudo-colonial. *Pseudo-* derives from the Greek word meaning to deceive or counterfeit. No deception was made or intended. Somewhere in the aesthetic genome was a Massachusetts Bay Colony cape that had shed its dormers and shingles and grown clapboard and a second story after being mated to a Center Hall Federalist dwelling where the center hall had atrophied to a coat closet inside the front door. Only one hearth remained and that was vestigial except on special occasions when the firewood Dad brought home filled the house with smoke.

Le Corbusier, foremost of the midcentury architectural theorists who wrecked the world's downtowns with glass tombstones and confined the poor in vertical concrete slums, had blandly called a house "a machine for living." Our parents were the avant-garde of Le Corbusier in blandness. My house was "a box for wife and family."

And a comfortable, cheerful, well-padded, and carefully placed box it was. The flaps were left open. As our generation is fond of saying, "We never locked the doors in the place where we grew up." That's not accurate. When night came and kids were in bed, moms and dads living in tediously safe locales went around turning deadbolts and fastening door chains. We think of them as unworried—smoking while pregnant, having one for the road before driving the family home, turning us loose in the backyard with lawn darts. But they did worry, in their generation's careful, limited way. They had certain firm ideas of what to worry about. They'd never had the opportunity to develop contemporary diverse, inclusive, free-range worry. They were more specifically anxious than we are, without the general anxiety. In this, their smoking and drinking certainly helped.

What our parents were most anxious for was us—first for us to be born and then for us to be happy and good. This is why they put so much effort into making sure the non-pseudocolonial house was in a good and happy place, the place where we grew up.

Now that we want our kids to be brilliant and successful we're free to move back to the city or out to Sedona or into mansion ghettos full of people with whom we are purposely strangers. Our parents hadn't learned to outsource their children's good and happy place.

They were ignorant of au pair supervision, the Suzuki method of early childhood stringed instrument instruction, math camp, and infant Pilates classes. They didn't know how to get us into private schools that accept only the top zero percent of applicants or sports programs reserved for those who will one day podium at the Olympics. Our parents needed a public place for us.

So we grew up in the suburbs, though with an experience somewhat different from what "grew up in the suburbs" would come to mean. I thought "car pool" was another swell new idea from GM.

Dad had the car at work. Mom's car was a used one, if it existed. If it didn't Mom took the bus. Grandma never learned to drive. She called a taxi. We rode our bikes. None of us was headed far. Suburbia hadn't yet expanded into a vast place where, our social critics tell us, there's nowhere to go and it's a long way to get there.

A great deal of thinking, mostly of the agonized kind, has been done about the effects of suburbanization on America. As if there were some hidden, cabalistic meaning in more nice homes and convenient places to work and shop. The meaning of the Baby Boom suburbs was that, because of depression and war, nobody had built any houses for a while and a lot of babies were being born.

Urban was still the meaningful part of the word *suburban*. People lived a driveway apart, back fence to back fence, with no lap pool enclosures or lap pools to be enclosed and no landscaping services trimming dense shrubbery screens. Streets retained their grid pattern. Each street was still called Such-and-Such Street rather than Suchand Drive or Andsuch Way. Dead ends had not yet gained the cachet of cul-de-sacs.

Suburban neighborhoods began a block or two from the city's shabby early-twentieth-century apartment buildings and paint-peeled Victorian piles now split into duplexes or rented by the room. Even where land was at no premium, out on the verge of town, a quarter-acre lot was a bit magnificent. And there were neighbors in the country too. Farms were smaller. Other farmhouses were within shouting distance.

Quite a few of our parents and most of our grandparents had grown up on such farms, either here or in some other country. This may be why the children of my neighborhood continued shouting. We seldom knocked on doors and never, except on Halloween, rang doorbells. When we wanted to contact a friend the accepted form was to stand outside his house and shout his name at the top of our lungs, "Oh, Bill*eeey*!," with the last syllable greatly prolonged and shrilly emphasized.

Children were forbidden independent use of the telephone. Any other form of personal communication technology, had it existed, would have been considered ridiculous. "Oh, Bill*eeey*!" could be heard a block and a half away. If a kid lived more than a block and a half away we didn't know him.

Adults themselves didn't use the telephone any more than necessary. Party lines were still common. Two rings for the Andersons, one ring for us. To say something on a party line was to tell the world. That it would be wonderful to tell the world one's every thought and feeling hadn't occurred to people yet.

Our house had a single phone, in the dining room on a shelf in a nook specifically designed to accommodate it. A call after 9 p.m. meant, at best, that someone in the family had died. Either that or the call had been prearranged, by mail, with my mother's sister in Chicago, to take advantage of lower nighttime long-distance rates. On long-distance calls Grandma shouted. It was, after all, a long distance.

People used to speak face to face. They did so in their own backyards over garden gates, as seen in ancient daily newspaper comic strips. Sometimes, in the background, there'd be a clothesline or a manually operated push lawn mower. People talked a lot, as an excuse to quit wrestling with wet bedsheets or stop shoving machinery through crabgrass. Of course, people still talk a lot, although what they're excusing themselves from now I don't know.

Anyway, when people spoke face to face sixty years ago they weren't also fiddling with their smartphones, facing other people's faces on Facebook when they were supposed to be facing you. And you weren't checking your e-mail and replying to your text messages when you were facing them. People had to speak directly to each other, paying attention to what they were saying and to what was being said. How they withstood the tedium I can't imagine.

In topics of conversation our parents ranged from bedsheets to lawn mowers. Would an automatic dryer send the electric bill through the roof? Those new rotary-style power jobs could take your whole foot off. I would listen in. For a moment, at the most. Sometimes there was good gossip between the moms. But the malice of children, like the malice of politicians, is an entirely public thing. We were not mature enough to enjoy a refined taste for private character assassination. (Nor, social media evidence indicates, are we yet.) Sometimes there was good sports talk between the dads. But a dad who knew enough about sports to be worth listening to would be playing in the major leagues. It was all we could do to get ours to play catch.

People used to write to each other. Any holiday departure, even to visit relatives in Ashtabula, occasioned picture postcards to all. The messages were sometimes jocular but never a joke, not even "Weather is here, wish you were beautiful!" And the pictures on the postcards were not ironic.

Irony, as a mode of communication, was well understood by our parents. They called saying the opposite of what is meant lying or being sarcastic. They used irony often but as a way to tell the world to piss off, not as a way to regard life, and certainly not as a way to say "hi" to friends and relations.

An extended separation, particularly from family, demanded frequent and voluminous correspondence. These missives were chatty, discursive, and brimming with minutiae. My mother and her sister wrote to each other once or twice a week. I have a packet of their letters. "Sewed the girls the *cutest* pair of matching aprons with pockets in the shape of Valentine hearts." "Tried Great Aunt Stella's recipe for oatmeal cookies, used oleo instead of lard."

These letters, more than half a century old, are remarkably like today's mom blogs. It's a subtle question what kind of progress has been made with human intercourse. In the bloggers' favor, they do talk about intercourse, which is interesting. In my mother's and aunt's favor, they didn't, which is a relief. To the credit of the bloggers, they make a desperate effort to entertain, however bitter and disappointed they may be. To the credit of Mom and Aunt Margie, they made a desperate effort to express no bitterness and disappointment, however entertaining that would have been.

Our parents lived in a world poised between intimacy and privacy, not one that paradoxically lacks both. My mother and my aunt were more boring than bloggers, but bloggers are boring everyone. My mother and my aunt bored only each other.

Even so, the Greatest Generation had tools of boredom that are little known these days. People used to "drop over"— unannounced, with children. Pretending not to mind was the neighborly thing to do. As was acknowledging the right of every neighbor who caught your eye to bend your ear. You had to have a good excuse to break off a conversation. Pretending that your barbecue grill was about to burn your house down might work, unless your neighbor sold home owner's insurance for a living.

Pretending had a lot to do with neighborliness. The neighborhoods of the 1950s were as make-believe as the Walt Disney Company's planned community, Celebration. But there was as yet no such job description as "imagineering." Our parents had to pretend without professional assistance, in their own unimaginative ways.

They came from farm villages, small towns, row houses, and tenements, all of which were snug and ethnic even when the ethnicity was an unspiced American mix of English, German, and Scots-Irish. Everybody was some kind of shirttail cousin or a friend of the family from way back or had jilted your dad's sister. The old neighborhoods were close-knit in an itchy, scratchy way. When everyone moved out it was a relief to all concerned.

In the new neighborhoods you didn't know the other people very well so you had the luxury of pretending to like them. Great store was put on neighborliness, meaning that you took a casserole next door if a neighbor had received a phone call after 9 p.m. And sometimes you dropped over unannounced, with children. People did indeed sit on the front porch and wave to other people sitting on other front porches. And they dutifully continued to do so until the minute a screened-in back porch was added to their house.

Children were the main victims of the neighborliness, one tenet of which was that every adult who lived in rough proximity to my house could give me the rough side of his or her tongue. Any childish transgression, actual or potential, was considered sufficient cause. Children were also the main perpetrators of the neighborliness, claiming all front yards and every backyard not occupied by a vicious dog as their commons. A garage with an unlocked door was likewise free space for kids, as were any tree branches, roofs, or porch decks that could be climbed onto.

We children were, of course, the whole cause of these neighborhoods. Houses were chosen strictly on the basis of price, price being determined by whether the neighborhood was a safe place to raise kids. Safety was measured by three standards. The first was the extent to which a given neighborhood's adolescents with ducktail haircuts were said to carry switchblades.

Once our parents had stretched their budget to find a location with the fewest alleged switchblades, they picked a particular house by making a complex calculation based on the likelihood of children getting run over on busy streets factored into the walking distance to the local grade school. (Incidentally, what old-fashioned parents thought of as walking distance to school was much longer than it is now, almost as long as what modern parents think of as a healthy morning run.) Then they checked to make sure the basement was dry. Wet basements gave children a cough. You could show our parents Buckingham Palace and all they'd say is "It's on a busy street" and "Does it have a dry basement?"

So we grew up in a good and happy place. And we were good. Or we were as good as kids were expected to be. We didn't suffer from childhood obesity, dyslexia, lactose intolerance, or behavioral disorders. We were husky, a little slow at reading, farted a lot, and were pains in the neck. Anyway, we were happy.

When I am grown to man's estate
I shall be very proud and great,
And tell the other girls and boys
Not to meddle with my toys.
—Robert Louis Stevenson,
                A Child's Garden of Verses

3

LIFE AS WE IMAGINED IT

Of course all childhoods are happy from a worry-burdened, regret-nagged, past-fifty, skinless-chicken-breast-for-dinner perspective. Or after three drinks. Then being a kid is a beautifully drawn scene suffused with bright primary colors and drenched in cheer, and I've gotten childhood mixed up with the illustrations in my old *Dick and Jane* reader.

But we in the Baby Boom *were* lucky. Children had once been put to work, if not in factories and farmyards then in the kitchens, cellars, and sculleries of their own homes. We were expected to clear our plates. And this could be finessed by carefully dawdling over our lima beans until *Kukla, Fran and Ollie* came on TV.

Now children have been put to work again. Homework started coming home with my children in kindergarten. Weekend assignment: learn to read. They work at private lessons in every sort of thing while I drive them around in a confusion of picking up kung fu and delivering "Kumbaya." After the work they do at the lesson, they practice the work they'll do at the next lesson. Recreation is organized according to the time management principles of workplace efficiency. Punch in, punch out. In the dread word *playdate* none of the pleasures of playing or dating are evoked. The kids work hard at sports, as well they should. Sports are an important part of the job of getting into exclusive schools. And while they're working on the essays that accompany the applications to those exclusive schools, the kids need to be well rounded. So they are drafted into volunteering for community service work. This begins at about age eight when the children are dragged to the local old age home to annoy the doddering elders with "Kumbaya" sing-alongs and demonstrations of kung fu technique. And it ends, if it ever does, with a postdoctoral unpaid internship at Save the Snakes.

How today's kids must yearn for the textile mills and milking stools of yore where they were occasionally left alone and could play tops with the spindles or have fun yanking the cow's tail.

Baby Boomers were excused from both the antique and the contemporary forms of youthful travail. *Kukla, Fran and Ollie* was on TV. Mom and Dad liked the show too.

For a few blissful years, between the time the *Enola Gay* landed and the time the helicopter parents took off, children were in control of childhood.

There were some rules. Everybody outdoors on nice days, no crossing busy streets, no hitting girls, no firecrackers in your mouth, come when you're called for dinner, and everybody indoors when the streetlights go on. These rules, like the definition of a "nice day," were broadly construed. They were enforced by the general committee of grown-ups with the inefficiency for which committees are famous. All eyes were upon us in the neighborhood but not looking too closely. And so we ran wild—in a rather tame manner.

What we did with our plentiful aggregation of playmates, our copious free time, and our minimal oversight was what right-minded kids have always done with freedom and opportunity. We wasted it. We did—according to the adult conception of doing something—nothing. We played.

I don't know that what or how we played differed much from playing as it's always been done. I wonder if play has differed since we were apes. Watching puppies and guppies and my children's baby gerbils I wonder if it's differed since we became vertebrates. The essence of play is to run around and squeal or, with guppies, bubble.

But it's hard to know to what extent there have been alterations in the nature of childhood play. Many authors have tried to recapture childhood (something that is interesting to real children only if it's done ludicrously as in the Harry Potter books). Yet authors must, perforce, make stories from the material of their youthful activities, leaving the rest of us who have been children feeling like Tom Sawyer's younger, duller brother, and you'll recall he had one.

True play exists outside the realm of plot. You can, if you like, give complication, climax, and denouement to a game of Kick the Can. But your tragic catharsis is going to be a flop unless you're telling a lot of lies. And people are liars about their childhoods, a trait they pick up from themselves as children. Even the youngest and most innocent children are unwilling to tell the truth about matters of childish importance. How boogers taste, for example.

Then we discover our private parts, learn to smoke, get driver's licenses, and forget the realities of childhood. Among the things I've forgotten are the rules for the games we played. I doubt I'd be a successful competitor in even Mother May I. But I'm not sure we remembered the rules at the time either. Arguing about a game's rules took longer than the game. And choosing up sides was of greater consequence than whether our side won.

Maybe the Baby Boom was showing its talent for what would become one of our most significant achievements, political impasse and standstill. Nobody thanks us for this now. But consider how the Baby Boom grew up in the aftermath of a period when politics had been doing anything but standing still, when politics had boldly trooped onto the field for a World War I and a World War II and was getting ready for a tripleheader. Not that we kids understood or minded this, but perhaps it affected us subliminally.

Or maybe we're just buttheads. Anyway, winning was not the point of Baby Boom games. We weren't much concerned with winning. Not that we subscribed to today's "everyone wins" ethos. The point of our games was failure. The fun of the thing was to tag some other kid and make him "it" or "poison" or "out" or to trip him or tackle him or bonk him with a ball. And her too. All run-around-and-squeal games were mixed sex. They were conducted with a total lack of consideration for the feelings of others that would be the envy of any modern child.

The same games still exist but they are conducted in day care, rec centers, and play groups under the tutelage of trained physical activity directors who do remember the rules. Winning is still not the point. Sensitivity is. They probably play Inclusion Tag. "We are all it." Total lack of consideration for the feelings of others has become too valuable to be wasted on kids. The media make billions from it.

Boys and girls ran around and squealed together, but outdoor games requiring greater concentration and precision were gender specific. In my neighborhood jacks was played only by girls, though the hand-eye coordination gained would have been more useful to boys with their ball sports. Marbles was played only by boys, though girls would have better appreciated the prettiness of the cat's-eyes, mibs, and clearys. Thus the stage was set for dissatisfaction with traditional ideas of masculine and feminine. No doubt Simone de Beauvoir mentions mibs and clearys somewhere in *The Second Sex*.

The chalk outline for hopscotch was drawn on the sidewalk by girls, but there was no shame in a boy playing. It was our first inkling that girls are better at anything to which they choose to turn their hand or, in this case, foot. We already knew from school that girls were less foolish. Sometimes a boy would foolishly jump rope with the excuse that boxers did it. What girls pull in Double Dutch is excellent preparation for divorce court. Parcheesi, Chutes and Ladders, Clue, Old Maid, Crazy Eights, and 52 Pickup were for rainy days, and if it looked like the rain was never going to stop we'd get out Monopoly. Despairing of its page upon page of rules we'd make our own. This is how both Wall Street investment strategy and Washington economic policy were invented by our generation. We also invented selling "Get Out of Jail Free" cards to the highest bidder. And we made deals with each other that were so complex that by the time six hotels had been placed on Baltic Avenue none of us had any idea what we were doing. This is the origin of the derivatives market and the real estate bubble. Climate change may not be all bad. The twenty-first-century financial climate was caused by too much rain in the 1950s.

Most of our play, however, had nothing to do with games. We liked games but we looked down on them, or we thought we should. Later we'd make "playing games" a pointed insult.

Games by their nature have limits. Games cramped our imagination. Imagination was something parents, Captain Kangaroo, Howdy Doody, the Mickey Mouse Club Mouseketeers, and other voices of authority were always urging us to use. Members of the Greatest Generation were terrible hypocrites about imagination. They refused to use theirs except as a way to create the dullest imaginable life for themselves. Then they turned around and insisted we use ours.

"The sky's the limit!" was one of those phrases bruited about by adults to children sixty years ago. Maybe the adults were beginning to wonder whether, and in what way, they'd reached for it themselves. "Dream big!" our third-grade teacher would say, which was ridiculous coming from someone who ended up teaching third grade. But we didn't know better. So the sky was the limit, to our limited ability to make it so, and we dreamed big, in our own small way.

What we did was make things up. Actually we didn't. We appropriated characters, circumstances, situations, and settings. Then we engaged in that art form which has come to be so oddly praised, improv. We did so by indulging in that activity which has come to be so oddly deplored, acting out.

War was the crux of play among boys. There were six of us about the same age who lived at the same end of the block. Billy Stumf, a year older, was captain. I was lieutenant. Johnny MacKay and Steve Penske were a battalion. Bobby Stumf and Jerry Harris, a year younger, were reinforcements. Any boy from more than half a block away was an Axis Power.

Love was the crux of play among girls, or love's simulacrum, domesticity. We boys might have tried to avoid girls' play except that Susie Inwood, who lived next door, could whip any of us. Thus Bobby and Jerry and Johnny and Steve and Billy and I played House. One benefit was Susie's big comic book collection, a whole milk crate full. Thus, when a blanket had been draped over the swing set or the branches in a brush pile had been arranged to form the rafters of a home, we would sit on the upturned box designated as a couch and do a good imitation of husbands helping in the kitchen.

Not that there were any kitchens when we were playing House. We each had a mother to whose kitchen all of us could resort and demand a snack at any moment as long as that moment was not within half an hour of a designated mealtime.

It was a snack to astonish those who believe there's been a decline in the quality of childhood nutrition—a piece of commercial white bread covered in butter (the high-fat-content, salted kind) and liberally sprinkled with refined sugar.

This we ate in that kitchen and not in our "house." Nor did we, in our fictitious domicile, participate in any other household activities or perform any household chores. The point of playing House was for the girls to make up their minds about who was "mommy" and who was "daddy" and who was "baby." All these years later, as far as I can tell, they're still deciding.

Among the other forms of girls' play into which we were dragooned was Store. It was an opportunity to gather all the money from everybody's Monopoly games and arrange it by denomination in a shoe box. Then the shoe box full of Monopoly money would be misplaced, making the next game of Monopoly even more like the operations of today's Federal Reserve than it was already.

Nothing was ever bought or sold in Store. It was a reenactment of the attitude of shopping, a happy pastime. There was no choosiness or haggling or shortage of unreal goods. When we couldn't find the Monopoly money, we used our parents' ration tokens left over from World War II.

Sometimes the girls would build a lemonade stand by getting the boys to lay planks over sawhorses and the moms to make lemonade in the form of Kool-Aid that was usually grape flavored while the girls worked on the sign until all the grape Kool-Aid had been drunk by the boys. The lemonade stand was a virtual business.

There was a thing of Susie Inwood's conception called Flying Horses. We were flying horses. We indicated that we were flying by hooking our thumbs into our armpits and flapping our elbows. There was no point to our being flying horses. We ran around as usual although this time neighing instead of squealing. There was no drama to our being flying horses. Nothing threatened our felicity. We were as big as horses and we could fly. We adopted roles for no reason and acted them to no purpose. The case could be made that we created reality TV before we knew anything about reality or much (there were only three channels) about TV.

And in a harbinger of what would be a generational trademark, we were sometimes in the mood for dark, edgy black humor. Then we played School.

When it was just boys we played Robin Hood. Tomato stakes were quarterstaffs. We played Knights of the Round Table with picket fence slat broadswords and garbage can lid shields. After the garbage can lids were taken away from us the fence slats became dueling foils or, if Mr. Biedermeyer had left his outboard motorboat on its trailer in the driveway, pirate sabers.

We played Cowboys. This was the only time it was permissible for a boy over five to skip. Done with our hands held out in front of us, grasping the reins, it was called galloping. We played Indians, but our twig arrows and tree branch and package twine bows didn't amount to much. Indians turned out to be better at hurling beanpole lances at each other and scalping younger brothers with Scout knives, to the extent that the crew cuts of the period allowed for scalping.

We did not, however, play Cowboys and Indians. That this showed a nascent multicultural sensitivity is a nice thought. And Tonto did seem like a good guy, while the Lone Ranger was kind of silly. "Who was that masked man?" Well, who the heck else in the Texas Rangers goes around by himself wearing a mask? But, really, playing Cowboys and Indians would have required two kinds of role playing at once. Roping and branding buffalo? Fast-draw tomahawk duels? This would have been overcomplicated. Using our imagination was different than using our brain. A flight of fancy, once embarked upon, requires a dull consistency in the fanciful. Hence some of the longueurs in the later career of the Baby Boom, such as being entranced with *Mary Hartman, Mary Hartman* in 1976.

We played Superman and Superboy and Superdog as well, if Johnny MacKay's German shepherd couldn't manage to free itself from the pillowcase tucked under its collar. When we raised our arms above our heads, fingers extended and palms down, it was stipulated that we were soaring through the air. But once Superman had landed (a hop on one foot with arms crooked and fists clenched) we didn't know quite what to do with him. He was too super—nobody could fight him.

And fighting was our chief joy. We played war across the front yards, war in the local park, war indoors with foxholes behind the davenport and snipers at the top of the stairs. We were usually the marines, sometimes the army, but never the navy because sailors drowned instead of being dramatically wounded and bleeding to death while bravely urging our platoon to leave us behind and take the hill.

Sometimes we were the German army. Nazis were to be deplored but they had cool uniforms. Our part of the state had been settled by Germans, and most of our war veteran fathers had, perhaps not coincidentally, been stationed in the Pacific. The exception being Mr. Meinhoff across the street who was quick to point out that he'd fought on the Russian front. The Japanese sounded funny and wore funny uniforms with puttees and soup bowl helmets and were more fun to kill.

The six of us were all on one side in these wars. Not that there was another side. Combat was waged against never invincible, always invisible enemies.

After the wars there was War, on the living room rug or along the upstairs hall or in Mom's herbaceous borders, with lead soldiers. We had hundreds of lead soldiers. We made them ourselves. Billy Stumf's dad supplied the molds. My dad brought home tire weights from the dealership where he sold cars. Billy and I melted the lead in a ladle on an old hot plate in the basement workshop surrounded by paint thinner and wood shavings. Parents put a great premium on children quietly amusing themselves.

Soldiers that came out of the mold missing a leg or a rifle were painted blue. These were the French. We let Bobby paint them.

If Billy and Bobby and I had done a particularly good job of quietly amusing ourselves, Mr. Stumf would lead us up to the attic and show us a roll of banknotes he'd taken from the body of a Japanese soldier during the Battle of Okinawa. The bloodstains were an exciting dark brown.

Mr. Stumf also taught us how to make machine-gun noises by vibrating our tongues and how to yell "Die you rousy Amelicans!" and "Banzai!" in a Japanese accent. He served in the Korean War, too, where he was an artillery officer. I remember sitting on the lawn with Billy and Bobby while Mrs. Stumf read a letter from her husband at the front.

"Dear Ellen, We were shelling the Chicoms today and I wrote your name on a shell and Billy's and Bobby's names on another shell and our dog Sam's name on a third."

I don't know where the idea of the reticent vet came from, the combat soldier who never speaks of his battlefield experience. Our parents told war stories all the time, including my mother, who'd been in the Women's Marine Corps. She was a control tower operator at Cherry Point, North Carolina, and witnessed more carnage on the runway than most dads had seen overseas.

Our enthusiasm for fighting extended to snowball fights, water balloon fights, dirt fights where new houses were being built, and fruit and nut fights when crab apples and buckeyes were in season.

But only by accident, or an occasional ice ball, did anyone get hurt. The fighting rarely degenerated into "a fight." We would wrestle angrily or try to give each other a kick in the shins at the most. Knockdowns and dragouts were unusual among Baby Boom children.

This must have been our own doing. We rarely heard adults—male adults, anyway—voice sincere disapproval of boys slugging each other. "So hit him back," our dads would tell us. My grandfather would happily recount how, as a twelve-year-old mechanic's apprentice, he'd fight his way to work through the boys in the Polack, Hunky, and colored neighborhoods and fight his way back home at night. To us this seemed inconceivable or like something from several blocks away where the poor kids lived and boys slugged each other all the time. Being poor back then—like joining ROTC later—meant you weren't a real Baby Boomer.

I once threw a roundhouse right at Steve Penske. So unused to punching was I and so unused to ducking punches was he that I put my fist into the side of the house and he banged his head on the drainpipe.

And when the Vietnam War arrived only one of us, Bobby Stumf, went. The rest of us had excuses. Billy Stumf's spleen was ruptured from high school football. Steve Penske developed allergies. Johnny MacKay got migraines. Jerry Harris came down with asthma. We used our imagination.

"Maybe," he said hesitantly, "maybe there is a beast . . . What I mean is . . . maybe it's only us."

—William Golding,
Lord of the Flies

4

IN THE DOLDRUMS OF FUN

School, given the amount of childhood that's spent in it, should form a greater part of this picture. But it doesn't. School was just there, inexorable, inevitable, and almost escape-proof. In our childhood, school life held the place that real life would occupy in our adulthood. You could avoid school but only by doing things that were worse or had worse consequences such as getting sick or telling wild lies, the juvenile equivalents of dying or going to Promises Malibu.

There were public schools and Catholic schools, mostly indistinguishable except that in the latter you learned about the infinite mercy of the blessed Virgin Mary and got your knuckles whacked more often.

Schools were big buildings. They resembled fortifications or castles. But they had been carefully designed to avoid any suggestion of the romance associated with citadels, strongholds, and keeps. The windows were large, to give children plenty of the healthy sunlight that didn't use to cause skin cancer and lots of air during the climate change that happened only twice a year, spring and fall, instead of all the time. Through those large windows we learned what a wide and wonderful world it is and how much we'd love to be out in it.

Some of the massive public schools that were built in the first third of the twentieth century haven't yet been torn down or repurposed. But their windows have been replaced with insulated panels that leave just a slit of casements for students to peer through. And we wonder at the increase in childhood suicide rates.

School started at 8:30. Before the doors opened children were expected to form two lines, one for the boys and one for the girls. The boys pushed each other. The girls teased each other. We would have been better behaved if we'd been mixed together, but the people who insist on organizing life and the people who have no idea how life is organized were and always will be the same people.

Classrooms were well populated. I count forty-two children in my third-grade class picture. The teacher was, until junior high, invariably a woman, usually single, and alone at her station of command. Teachers' aides had not yet been sent to the aid of teachers. Busybody parents weren't sticking their noses in from the back row. Elected representatives of the school board weren't visiting to make sure that the curriculum was conformist, or that the curriculum was nonconformist, according to which kind of nut won the school board election. Not that our teachers needed such assistance. They wielded the kind of unalloyed power that God used to have in the Old Testament before 1950s Sunday school teachers got to Him.

Corporal punishment was not unknown in public schools. But its infrequency and the seemingly random nature of its application made it less a deterrent than a suburban legend. Paddling gave us a sort of campfire story to tell on the way home from school. "And then he was sent to the principal."

The more effective disciplinary measure was to send us to sit in the hall. A break from the crowded, busy classroom would have been a relief to a sensible generation, but we are a sensitive generation and can't stand to be isolated. The worst penalty we could devise, when we got children of our own, was give them a "time-out." Probably the tykes were thinking—like many people who have had experience with our generation—"Please, make it two."

Our teachers were not old bats by any means. Many were fresh from their El Ed major at state universities and full of innocent enthusiasm. Others were old bats. Pedagogical methods combined the hopelessly old-fashioned with the hopelessly newfangled. There was still copious rote learning and much copying of things from blackboards. We were made to memorize the alphabet both forward and backward, the latter being something I most certainly can't do to this day. I didn't have much success with the former either. When I use the dictionary I'm still singing the "ABC Song." My parents bought the 45 and I played it on a little red record player. I used to catch myself, among Y and Z words, mouthing the lyrics of the final verse—*Now I know my ABCs/Aren't you very proud of me?*—sometimes aloud, which occasioned looks in the college library.

We were taught to read with flash cards. "You can remember it's the word *look* because it has two eyes in the middle." This is not conducive to good spelling. It's no accident that SpellCheck is a product of the Baby Boom, and no accident that we misspelled "spell check." Anything to get out of liiking up words in the dictionary.

On the other hand, History and Geography had been replaced with Social Studies. By the end of grade school we were well prepared to go out and take Margaret Mead's place in Samoa, if we'd known where Samoa was. We studied the handicrafts, songs, and square dances of the American pioneers. We knew everything about frontier life except when it happened and why. There was a great fad for coonskin caps thanks to the Walt Disney show's Davy Crockett episodes, which were only slightly less historically inaccurate than Margaret Mead. We understood that pioneers wore coonskin caps. We didn't understand that they'd had to eat the raccoon first.

One lesson the Baby Boom did learn was that we were being bored on purpose. Until we understood school we regarded boredom as an accident—nobody to play with, nothing but *Name That Tune* on TV. At its worst, during Thanksgiving dinner with a relentlessly joshing Uncle Timmy, or on a visit to Grandma's ancient friend who was under the impression that children liked horehound candy, boredom was the result of mistakes in attempts to entertain us. Being boring was a fault, not a vice. It had never occurred to us that boredom could be premeditated.

*   *   *

Our generation does not believe in original sin. But we do believe that Adam and Eve were boring. We take it on faith that humankind has fallen from divine enjoyment of life. We carry the burden of blasé and are continually tempted to ennui in thought and deed. We can be restored to an Edenic state only by the grace of the Interesting.

We know this from school and from Sunday school, Scouting, summer camp, and organized sports. If you weren't bored by these institutions and activities, you weren't paying attention.

Let us not commit an intentional fallacy. The grown-ups bored us. They had a purpose for doing so. Therefore they bored us on purpose. That is not to say they *meant* to bore us. Quite the contrary with Sunday school teachers, who tried everything to make religion entertaining. God, how they failed.

The tedium of Sunday school, though less frequent and prolonged than the tedium of school, produced greater hopelessness and despair. It was a theft from the heavenly gift to us kids, the weekend. In church basements all over America the gospel of Mark 10:14 was being invoked, "Suffer the little children to come unto me," leaving little children wondering what they'd done to deserve the suffering (". . . and the children shall rise up against their parents," Matthew 10:21, but that verse was never taught).

Jesus should have been frighteningly interesting. He was undead. He wore his bathrobe outdoors. He had a beard. The halo thing meant he glowed in the dark. But by the time the Sunday school teachers were finished with Him all the gee whiz had been taken out of Jesus. He was always patient, kind, gentle, and understanding. The people we knew who were like that were really dull, except Mom. And Mom would give us hell sometimes while Jesus, we were told, was giving us the other place.

The glory of the other place was so vaguely described that it's easy to understand why our generation would mistake getting high on drugs for it.

Hell should have been fascinating. But the Sunday school teachers explained it as a sort of absence, without an excuse, from meeting God. Meeting God, this sounded worrisome. But hell went on forever. This sounded like Sunday school.

Despite my name, both my parents were milquetoast Protestants. The O'Rourkes had been Catholic but in the 1920s my widower grandfather divorced his lunatic second wife. She'd put her stepchild—my dad's baby brother, later to become overjocular Uncle Timmy—out on the back steps in the snow as punishment for wetting his pants. His underwear froze.

The Catholic Church refused to grant an annulment. Granddad got so angry that he joined the Freemasons, the Republican Party, and the Lutheran Church, all in one day. It's a family story that is, as we journalists say, too good to check. Mom came by her Presbyterianism honestly.

During the 1950s denominations of the Lutheran, Presbyterian, Methodist, and Episcopalian kind had fitted the Light of the World with a lampshade so it wouldn't produce distracting salvational glare and dampened the fires of perdition to avoid spiritual smoke inhalation. A stillness of the soul and a quiet reverence during church services had been turned into sitting still and being quiet.

Catholic kids had the advantage of scary nuns, still in full habits. Did they have hair? Did they have *feet*? Priests, performing the mumbo jumbo of the Latin Mass, were almost as impressive as stage magicians. A Catholic priest could probably pull a quarter out of your ear. (That he could do something else in some other place of yours was not yet a popular article of faith.) And saints were all over the place with special powers like comic book superheroes but more numerous and more outlandishly costumed although beset with really a lot of Kryptonite causing them to be martyred all the time.

And there were kids, like Johnny MacKay, who went to the other kind of Protestant church, the kind in a cement block building with a clever sign out front.

CH RCH TODAY
WHAT'S MISSING?
U ARE

Never mind that much of the congregation and maybe the preacher hadn't finished high school, here was learning and culture. Worshippers were the heirs of Jonathan Edwards, one of colonial America's great religious thinkers, and conversant with the brilliant prose style of his "Sinners in the Hands of an Angry God." "Consider the fearful danger you are in: 'tis a great furnace of wrath, a wide and bottomless pit, full of the fire of wrath . . . you hang by a slender thread, with the flames of divine wrath flashing about it . . . ." Their religion had special effects.

My religion had specific evasions. The more specific the query I made, the more evasive was the response. How come Santa isn't in the crèche at Christmas? Baby Jesus is getting presents from the Three Wise Men but nothing from Santa? Does the Easter Bunny come before or after Jesus rises? When the rock was rolled back was the candy inside or outside the tomb? What does the Holy Ghost dress up as on Halloween?

Baby Boomers mock born-agains (or we do until we get cancer, go to jail, or reach the "Higher Power" part of the 12-step program). But Christian fundamentalists can answer these questions and we can't.

Scouting was Sunday school with mission creep. There was God *and* Country and for some reason both were in the Great Outdoors. The proper way to show respect for God and Country when They were outdoors was to adopt pseudo-military dress and behavior.

We liked wearing the uniforms until we realized, immediately, that they looked stupid. We did not actually go outdoors much. Most Scouting was done in the church gymnasium, but at least it was on a weeknight. I remember maybe three camping trips in my five years of desultory participation in the Boy Scouts. It rained.

"Boy Scout" was not a term of endearment among the Greatest Generation. They'd had enough of military dress and behavior, pseudo- or otherwise. There was no superabundance of dads volunteering to be Scoutmasters. Organizational details were left to high school–aged Eagle Scouts who didn't—even we could tell—have much of a life at high school.

Cub Scouts got no male supervision at all. Den Mothers did their best. As a crafts project for our den, Johnny

MacKay's mother chose painting china figurines of choirboys. She had the figurines glazed in the kiln belonging to Mrs. Furstein who lived one block over and was arty. I don't think this was what Baden-Powell had in mind.

When we graduated to the Boy Scouts proper there was the knot tying. What a tangled skein of cordage had to do with God and Country was not clear. What was to be done in the Great Outdoors with a big snarl of rope wasn't clear either. Study of the classics was not a strong point in 1950s education. If we'd known the legend of Alexander the Great and the Gordian knot we would have used our Scout knives on something besides our little brother's hair and sliced right through the hopeless clumps of failed half hitches, sheet bends, and bowlines. Or, anyway, we would have cut ourselves free from the Boy Scouts. As it was, the knottiness prefigured a generational tendency to find the most complex solutions to our problems. Health care reform, variable rate subprime mortgages, and Microsoft Word come to mind.

First aid was also taught. If you need it you'd better hope someone my age doesn't get to you first. And there were weak attempts to memorize semaphore flag signals and do other things that didn't engage our attention, followed by Battleball.

Steve Penske and I were charged with forming a new patrol. We chose the name Bat Patrol. We had the coolest patrol badge. Our patrol's call was an "EEEEEE," inaudible to human ears.

We weren't any good at going to summer camp either, as Woodstock was to prove. Summer camp was basic—leaky forest, dense cabins, mucky mess hall, and a lake that smelled like greasy food. In time our generation would become fans of the primitive, the rustic, the crude, and the clumsily handmade. But not when our parents were paying for it.

We played Capture the Flag at summer camp. The point of the game was to lose the unpopular kids in the woods. At my camp everyone was unpopular.

Summer camp was an exercise in doing things we didn't want to do with people we didn't know. A nature hike with a bunch of strangers was a lot like going to work. We in the Baby Boom put that off for as long as we could, but when we did go to work—on politics, finance, media, and the Internet—we did so with such a will that we almost wrecked the country, so summer camp must have been a suitable preparation.

Organized sports, as they were foisted upon us, had only a tenuous relationship to real sports, the kind we and our dads rooted for on radio and television. My friends and I didn't make a mental connection between Little League and the Cleveland Indians or even between Pop Warner football and the athletic glories on display from September through Thanksgiving in our local high school stadium.

Part of the problem was the fan base. Our parents didn't come down from the stands at our games and hit coaches, opposing players, and each other in swell melees that went viral and got, like, a million hits on YouTube. Such behavior was inconceivable. It would have meant that our parents had come to our games.

Our parents were home getting a little peace and quiet while sports "kept us out of trouble." Meanwhile, we could imagine ourselves as sports stars, but not while playing under adult supervision. There was too much supervising. We had just crossed the finish line and won the Indianapolis 500 in our Soap Box Derby racer when somebody yelled, "Fly ball, you dummy!"

Our parents imagined us as sports stars, too, when they bothered to take time off from imagining sports were keeping us out of trouble. (That playing sports is a way to meet kids who are real trouble is something we never told Mom and Dad.) Our parents imagined, "If the kid has talent maybe he'll get a scholarship to Youngstown State." But even if the dream came true, sports were regarded as a likely road to an income in the high four figures teaching gym someplace with the summer off for standing in the weeds at a public park yelling, "Fly ball, you dummy!"

We suffered from an emphasis on good sportsmanship. We weren't allowed to pump our fists in the air, exchange high fives, do sack dances, or prance around in the end zone as if we had Deep Heat in our jockstraps. We were reduced to bragging to smaller children out of adult earshot. (And the purchase of a first jockstrap was a painful humiliation. Our mothers hovered nearby. The size we required was invariably "small.")

We worshipped our sports heroes, collected their bubble gum pack baseball cards, followed their exploits in the sports pages as well as we could in the balderdash of sports writing, and argued about whether, if Rocky Marciano played baseball and Mickey Mantle was a boxer, who would win. We worshipped our sports heroes, but we didn't identify with them. Wearing an imitation item of Stan Musial's uniform to school would have been as odd as wearing

Batman's cape. We'd be laughed at. And sent home. Maybe pro athletes are more approachable in the guilty minds of boys now that "felony indictment" has become a sports statistic.

We were never asked whether we liked sports. Some of us did. Billy and Bobby Stumf were good at sports. For the rest of us . . .

"Pat's batting. Everybody move in!"

"Jerry's on your team. He was on our team last time."

"Bobby, run the buttonhook. Billy, fall back and pass. And Steve and Johnny, you two, uh, go deep."

Liking sports wasn't the point. But, the adults informed us, being good at sports wasn't the point either. This left quite a few of us wondering, "What's the point?"

The point was to learn teamwork and leadership. The Greatest Generation was big on teamwork. I can't think why. They'd just lost China with their Chiang Kai-shek team, been stalemated in Korea on the UN team, and were in the middle of a Cold War that was the result of having been former teammates with the Soviet Union. When corporations teamed up it was called a monopoly and needed to be stopped with antitrust laws. When workers teamed up it was called Jimmy Hoffa and needed to be investigated by the FBI. But out on the sports field we were told, "There is no 'I' in team." And what with the way we were taught to spell in the 1950s, we had to think about that one.

Our parents were also big on leadership while, at the same time, being grossly cynical about leaders. They would say things like, "Ike wanted to be president because then he'd get *two* pensions when he retired." They'd impute base motives to those in positions of even the least authority. "The paperboy knows the Ryans are on vacation so he delivered their paper to us and saved himself three cents." And they knew what happened to youthful leaders. Our parents remembered D-day. They themselves were experts in "leading from behind," preferably from behind a beer at home while we played Little League. Maybe all generations want their children to have what they did not. Or maybe they didn't love us as much as we think.

The point of organized sports was teamwork and leadership. As far as I could tell from questioning adults, the point of everything they cajoled us into doing—sports, Scouting, religious instruction, summer camp—was teamwork and leadership.

I wonder what kind of leader I was supposed to become by getting beaned at home plate, making granny knots, being paired on the buddy system in the lake at camp with a kid who ran away and hid in the latrine, and thinking up three questions to ask Jesus if He came to our church bake sale. And I wonder what kind of team would want a semiconscious, tangled-up, soaking-wet, agnostic team member.

When you hear, these days, that there's no teamwork or leadership in Congress, the White House, business, industry, education, civil society, or at home when it's time to decide who's making dinner, it's because the Baby Boomers would rather have been watching TV. Even *Name That Tune*.

And, by the way, why is it that the TV of the 1950s, along with the suburbs and the tail fins, takes so much grief from deep thinkers? In a 1961 speech the chairman of the

Federal Communications Commission, Newton N. Minow (now *there's* a name for a deep thinker), told the National Association of Broadcasters, right to its face, that television was "a vast wasteland." As if, before TV, my family spent the evening playing chess and Tchaikovsky. *Leave It to Beaver* is still taking a beating as the exemplar of all that's tepid and bogus in our Baby Boom cultural heritage. This pleasantly written and acted diversion featured a masterful portrayal of Silent Generation Iago Lite in Eddie Haskell. Is the depiction of middle-class Baby Boom life in *Leave It to Beaver* less acute and penetrating than the depiction of middle-class Elizabethan life in Shakespeare's *Merry Wives of Windsor*? Which entertainment winks more often at moral turpitude? And, tell the truth, which would you rather sit through?

Not to go off on another digression (although the Baby Boom has always been inclined to wander from the main subject whenever we can get a hall pass), but unfounded objections to tract houses, DeSotos, and Beaver Cleaver make you fear for the mental well-being of intellectuals. We are not a highly intellectual generation and who can blame us.

Baby Boom girls didn't mind the boredom as much as Baby Boom boys. Girls could see into the future. This was evident in the way girls played with dolls that had dollhouses full of sinks, toilets, bassinets, and other items of real futurity plus doll clothes and somebody's older brother from down the block who'd rip Barbie's blouse off to look at her breasts. Meanwhile boys were playing with one-legged lead soldiers that were French.

Girls knew that the tedium of school was a necessary preparation for the tedium of home and family. And Baby Boom girls had an intuition that their tedium would extend beyond home and family to professions, corporate management, and the State Department. They'd better get ready to be bored.

Boys were driven crazy—literally crazy, as defined in the current edition of the American Psychiatric Association's *Diagnostic and Statistical Manual of Mental Disorders*. The "diagnostic criteria" for Attention Deficit Hyperactivity Disorder include:

- makes careless mistakes in schoolwork
- does not seem to listen
- is often easily distracted
- fidgets with hands or feet or squirms in seat
- runs about or climbs excessively
- has difficulty playing or engaging in leisure activities quietly

These boys have been accurately diagnosed as boys. Now there are drugs to treat it. The medications are what Baby Boomers would call uppers. The recommended therapy for ADHD is, essentially, dating fat girls to get their diet pills to study for exams.

It's a shame, although not because Ritalin, Adderall, Vyvanse, Concerta, and whatever lead to a lifetime of drug dependency and squalor. I came of age in the 1960s. A lifetime of drug dependency and squalor has its points. But kids are sitting still after the bell, engrossed in their schoolwork, and being denied the benefits of the fantasy life induced by utter boredom.

*   *   *

Our school's classrooms and halls had two-tone paint based on some theory that was current about what was good for eyesight: a pale bile green above a nose-high watermark with a darker cheese mold green below. The school is filling up with water, right to the watermark level. Miss Burbage's big wooden desk and chair are floating away and Miss Burbage with them. We have to tread water or we'll drown. "Get back in your seat," says Miss Burbage.

Our school is indeed a fortress. Other kids from other schools are attacking it. We rain Miss Burbage's potted African violets down upon their heads. They break through the girls' entrance with a teeter-totter battering ram. We fence with wooden rulers. They throw blackboard erasers. Our only hope is to retreat to the auditorium and barricade the stage with cardboard straw, cardboard twigs, and cardboard bricks from the first grade's performance of *Three Little Pigs*. "Get back in your seat," says Miss Burbage.

My desk is a helicopter. Mary Ritter sits in front of me. Her dual braids spin, *whup, whup, whup.* Jack Gertin sits behind me, a round boy, the tail rotor. I have twin .50-caliber Number 2 pencils. Oh no, ack-ack at twelve o'clock high. Good thing I've got a parachute in my book bag. "For the last time," says Miss Burbage, "get back in your seat."

And every couple of months we'd have a real air-raid drill and get under our desks to protect ourselves from nuclear holocaust. Nowadays the kids, their minds made literal by drug-induced obsession with doing long division, would be scared they were going to die. But we, in the sure and certain hope of fantasy life, knew that atomic bombs only killed grown-ups and probably caused school to be let out early. Billy and I and Johnny and Steve and Bobby and Jerry would survive, like in *Lord of the Flies* but without the flies. Not that I'd read the book, or heard of it. But when I did read it I was impressed anew with the capacity of adults like William Golding to spoil things.

One boy is almost as good as a man. Two boys are half as good as a man. Three boys are useless.
                                                    —New Hampshire saying

5

MERE ANARCHY IS LOOSED

Adulthood, however, pursues the most evasive child. And he stumbles upon such trip-ups as the facts of life. These were put in my way by cousin Stuart on a visit from Chillicothe. Stuart was a forthright and plain-minded sixth grader not known to tease or fib. I had previously imagined—with the help of parental vagueness—something like a bacterial infection communicated by love and marriage. Mom's tummy got a germ, which was in the air, from Dad.

Stuart told me what part of Dad went where in Mom (or approximately where). I was an unbeliever, firm in my sexual atheism. Stuart protested, "It's true!" Then he added, more sympathetically, "You'll get used to the idea." He said,

"Eventually you'll even want to do it yourself with your wife." Although he didn't sound fully convinced about this last part.

I was puzzled by the mechanics of the thing. How did this limp member get stuffed into that appointed place? (A prescient concern, but I was getting ahead of myself by half a century.) I had erections at the time but I didn't connect them with sex. They seemed to be some pleasurable version of an injury causing stiffness and swelling. I worried a bit about erections. We had a leg-humping toy fox terrier called Pee Wee with a penis that was rigid and ready two-thirds of the day. I asked my mother what was wrong with Pee Wee. "He's nervous," she said. Then I worried a bit about what was making me nervous.

It wasn't the facts of life themselves, although these did present a conundrum. Mothers and fathers performed the business to produce a baby. My sisters were twins. Had my parents done it twice? Or had they done it *three times*?

Such questions were not cleared up by the sex education of the day, of which there was none. Looking into contemporary sources such as the supposed bible of 1950s parenting, *Baby and Child Care* by Dr. Benjamin Spock, I see a call for giving children frank and factual information about sexual matters. Women's magazines, newspaper advice columnists, teachers, and parents seemed to agree. They also seemed to agree not to listen to themselves. Thus, for boys at least, Dad took us aside and mumbled, "Boys and girls are different, and your mom and I are the same. That is, I mean, we're different too, and . . ." After that he pretty much ground to a halt. There was a long pause. Then he blurted, "Isthereanythingyouwantmetotellyou?"

To which we answered, "No." This, translated from boy-speak, meant, "Oh, God, no! No, no, no! Please shut up!"

Mothers must have had more substantial conversations with daughters, if for no other reason than that the girls would be bleeding from a surprising place every month. Or perhaps moms were no better than dads. My high school girlfriend told me she learned all she knew about menstruation from the back of her mother's Kotex box.

At any rate the details of screwing were obscure. The dirty word itself was confusing. I don't know what the girls were saying to each other, but the boys were engaged in various debates. There was, for example, the "How many holes?" argument. This was conducted atop Steve Penske's backyard swing set, which had been relegated to a place to climb up and perch on because we considered ourselves too mature to use the swings.

The debates were brief and halfhearted. Sex was disgusting but not disgusting enough to pique a boy's full interest. A "sail cat" was really disgusting. Sometimes in hot weather on a busy road a cat would be hit by a car and repeatedly run over until it was flattened and baked dry on the asphalt. Then the cat could be peeled up and sailed through the air. Toward the end of the 1950s the Wham-O company began marketing the Frisbee, or "Pluto Platter," as it was originally called. The patent holder, Walter Morrison, claimed he got the idea from pie tins he used to toss around on the beach in the 1930s. Any experienced boy could have debunked that story.

Since sex and the Frisbee would become totems of the Baby Boom there must be some connection. I can only say that the whole use and entire purpose of the sail cat was to toss it at girls.

*   *   *

Nowadays the first glimmerings of puberty lead to the behavior for which puberty was naturally and organically designed. This is a cause of shock and horror to modern parents who are otherwise worshipful of all things natural and organic. Or so I gather from the media. My wife and children are tactfully mum on the subject.

Back then the first glimmerings of puberty led to mayhem among boys, the sail cat being just the beginning. I suppose this was sublimation. Sublimation doesn't exist anymore, or so I gather from the media. But it was still extant in the 1950s when we channeled forbidden sexual impulses into acceptable activities. The activity we accepted with the most enthusiasm involved another product from the Wham-O company, its slingshot. A good slingshot loaded with a half-inch steel ball bearing was, at close range, potentially as lethal and probably as accurate as a 9mm Glock. And every boy was licensed to carry.

In fairness it should be said that it never occurred to us to use our slingshots to settle personal grudges let alone rob drugstores. And half-inch steel ball bearings were hard to come by and heavy in the pocket. Our usual ammunition was the cat's-eyes, mibs, and clearys left over from our marbles-playing days. And we only shot at each other for fun.

A particularly good game on summer nights was for one of us to crouch in my backyard while the other boys with their slingshots were stationed four doors down on the second-floor airing deck above the Stumfs' back door. The solitary hero had to climb over our chain-link fence, belly-crawl through a weed-strewn empty lot, do a broken field run across the open space behind the Inwood and MacKay houses with only Johnny's aging German shepherd for cover, then make his way over the hedges and through the elaborate gardening of the crabby old people who lived next door to the Stumfs. The old people must have had a hundred rose-bushes. Fortunately wearing shorts was unthinkable for any boy over eight. Meanwhile the airing-deck defenders kept up a continual barrage, and their attacker returned fire as best he could until he reached the protective overhang at the Stumfs' back steps. His last act of bravado was to step out from under this revetment and loose a Parthian shot, which broke a window, and we all caught hell.

Breaking a window was the great taboo for the armed boy. According to modern adult lore the constant scold of our childhood was "You'll put somebody's eye out!" I don't recall parents ever saying so. They were too worried about us breaking windows. And rightly. Windows seemed to break more easily in those days. Every ball sport was accompanied by the sound of shattering glass. I even managed it while *pretending* to play football. I was in our upstairs hall kicking the winning extra point against Notre Dame after the fourth-quarter-and-seconds-to-go Ohio State touchdown. My shoe came off and went through the window at the top of the stairs.

The window situation got worse as boys advanced in their projectile capabilities. We had slingshots and BB guns and artillery of our own invention such as the firecracker-powered frozen juice can and the discovery that a Louisville Slugger could send a half-inch steel ball bearing about a mile.

The boys from one block over were more enterprising. They took expended metal CO_2 cartridges, the kind used in seltzer bottles, and packed them with match heads. Then they found a length of pipe with a suitable diameter and crimped one end. The result was a spectacular little rocket launch with a charred CO_2 cartridge reentering the earth's atmosphere two or three neighborhoods away where it doubtless broke a window. The twelve-year-olds buying four or five hundred books of paper matches at the local cigar store were regarded with equanimity by its owner. One young man went too far, however, and broke open a couple of his dad's shotgun shells and replaced the match heads with gunpowder. He was treated in the emergency room (we all knew the place), and I believe he had to go without TV for a week.

If someone had asked us—and no one did—why we went everywhere carrying slingshots, BB guns, Scout knives, M-80s, and other weaponry, we would have said we were hunting squirrels.

This was an acceptable premise. The bowl of human compassion had not yet overflowed and begun to shower its blessings on nature in general and certainly not on squirrels. It was a crueler age.

Concentrating the sun's rays on an anthill with a magnifying glass and watching the ants pop was regarded as a wholesome pastime, like tennis. Our favorite use for tennis rackets was to swat wasps, though not the kind that build big paper hives and have a lot of angry compatriots. We took our tennis rackets to the scruffy lawn of Johnny MacKay's cement block church where sand wasps made their solitary nests between tufts of chickweed.

The sand wasp lives down an ominous hole and grows to an immensity, nearly two inches in length and thick as a finger. Billy Stumf, a convincing boy (he grew up to be a boat salesman), claimed its sting was lethal. We would hover as though hung upon a slender thread over the bottomless pit full of fire and wrath and a sand wasp. Then—no doubt improving our serves and backhands—we'd volley the bug into oblivion.

What went on with frogs and fireworks does not bear description, but I have a friend my age who is convinced that when he arrives at the Pearly Gates an immense bullfrog will be there brandishing a huge bottle rocket and staring with grim relish down my friend's throat.

We never did get any squirrels, the scampering jerks. They were too hard to hit even when we resorted to the explosive slingshot team. One boy would grip the slingshot handle in both fists. A second boy would put a cherry bomb in the sling and pull back the elastic to its fullest extent. And a third boy would light the wick. Jerry Harris was a fumbler with matches and slow to yell, "Fire!" I had some explaining to do about the singe holes in my T-shirt. Ruining your clothes was considered grave misbehavior.

We had our moral limits. We would never harm a dog. Even the mangiest stray excited our sympathy. We immediately went to our respective kitchens to get something to feed it, causing all our mothers to rush out waving brooms and flapping aprons to chase the poor thing away. It was gospel among midcentury adults that the first thing a dog did when it got lost was catch rabies.

And we wouldn't hurt a cat. In the daytime. Any cat found out-of-doors after dark was an enemy to boyhood and sworn prey. We hunted them with our Wham-Os, Daisy air rifles, and firecrackers down alleys, over garbage cans, and between garages. But our incompetence equaled our evil, and I think the most we bagged was an outraged caterwaul. Actually, the cats got the better of us. Having chased a tabby into the eighteen-inch-wide passageway separating the Stumfs' garage from the Penskes', Johnny MacKay let fly with a whole string of lit one-inchers that ricocheted off the eaves, landed at his feet, and left him deaf for a week. Not that his parents noticed since all a boy ever said to his parents was "Huh?"

We had better luck hunting lawn ornaments. Birdbaths, garden gnomes, and glass gazing balls were deemed a challenge to our honor. What kind of timid, weakling boys did people think we were to leave such quarry unguarded in their yards? What sort of clumsy poachers and bad shots did they believe us to be? There's a joyful ringing clash and a beautiful splay of mirrored shards when a glass gazing ball gets a half-inch steel ball bearing smack in the middle on a moonlit night.

People, as well as animals and things, were fair game, as long as they were defenseless. Crabby old people who lived by themselves were tormented. Their doorbells were stuck to a permanent buzzing with thumbtacks. Their windows were soaped. And in the most extreme case I remember, involving the rose-growing Stumf neighbors, a paper bag full of dog poop was placed on a front porch and set on fire with the idea that the crabby old people would come out and stamp on the flames. But the dog poop was wet and the blaze died.

It was not a good time to be a younger brother. Although parents kept that particular torturing somewhat in check by making our backsides fair game too. It was truly not a good time to be an unusual kid. There was a slight boy at our school, precise in his speech and fastidious in his manners, whose mother had him in a ballet class. His life was hell. Being fat was an offense, unless you were friends with the fat kid, and even then, if Jerry Harris goofed up, it was possible for all of us to turn on him.

Fatty, fatty, two-by-four,
Couldn't get through the outhouse door.

We're proud of ourselves, as a morally attuned generation, for creating a kinder society, more empathetic and caring, more accepting and less judgmental. And it's fair to say we've done so. But we were careful not to become better people until we'd had our fun.

When not wreaking havoc on the pets, possessions, or persons of others, we endeavored to wreak it on ourselves. All sports were contact sports. Tackle basketball was the norm beneath the hoop mounted over every garage door. In baseball it was considered unsporting to steal second without sliding at full speed, cleats first, straight at the second baseman even if he was nowhere near second base. The point of sandlot football was to knock everybody to the ground. Carrying, throwing, and kicking the football were beside the point. Jerry Harris ran me down (the sedentary nature of childhood obesity had not yet been discovered), tackled me, and broke my arm while I was playing defensive linebacker.

We cherished our bicycles as a way to get around but also, at least as much, as a way to get hurt. A careless dismount could do the job, smacking our testicles against the crossbar. That crossbar marked our bicycle as a "boy's bike." There were boys, burdened by older sisters and frugal parents, who rode a "girl's bike," with a step-through frame. They might as well have been wearing the skirts the step-through frame was designed to accommodate.

We rode our bikes down the steepest slopes (not very steep in our part of the Midwest). We rode our bikes around corners at the highest speed (about ten miles per hour on our single-sprocket Schwinns). Our favorite way to hurt ourselves was playing "chicken." Two furiously pedaling boys rode toward each other to see who would swerve. There was, however, a tacit agreement between us that each had flinched last. Imaginative as we were, we lacked the fictional skill to invent a story for parents explaining how we both managed to wreck our bikes at the same place at the same time. Nonetheless we considered ourselves daredevils, a term of great approbation.

Daredevil was a word to which we might have given some thought, inasmuch as the best place to play chicken was the empty parking lot of Johnny MacKay's fire-and-brimstone church where the sand wasps made their nests.

How we really got hurt was by accident, trying to bring our bikes to abrupt halts on loose gravel. We never understood the physics of this maneuver.

I blame Tarzan for our ignorance of physics. The old Johnny Weissmuller movies were on TV almost every Saturday morning. Tarzan swung effortlessly on his jungle vine pendulum, from wherever he was to wherever he wanted to go, with no thought of pivot point, length of pendulum arc, or pendulum acceleration back to equilibrium position. We would do the same on a rope from a tree branch in the Penske backyard to the roof of the Penske garage, making the Tarzan yodel and trying to thump ourselves on the chest with one hand while holding onto the rope with both. Pendulum acceleration back to equilibrium position was smack into the Penske tree trunk.

But whatever ignorance of physics we indulged in, extra glory went to anyone who required a bandage larger than those that came in the standard Band-Aid box.

*   *   *

Meanwhile, what were the girls doing? I don't know. Boys didn't notice. Boys didn't notice anything that wasn't loud, fast, or about to explode. The girls were too old to make those high-pitched shrieks of glee or grief that could be heard all over the neighborhood. (The raised voices of mothers and daughters didn't carry much beyond bedroom walls and certainly not all the way back to the alley where we were skewering newts on lit sparklers.) The girls were too young to be "fast," as it was still called. And the girls weren't married to us yet, so we didn't make them explode.

It used to be that, toward the end of childhood, boys and girls led separate lives. There was a kind of half-joking purdah. On one side of the veil frilly dress patterns were sewn and stuffed animals were collected. On the other side Johnny and Bobby and I were given hammers and crowbars and five dollars apiece to spend a glorious afternoon tearing down the MacKays' rickety one-car garage. We didn't drop the roof right on our heads, but not for lack of trying. Boyhood and girlhood were parodies of manhood and womanhood.

As our generation got older we ceased to be amused by the joke. By the time we'd grown up the list of things women aren't supposed to do was reduced to using the men's room unless the line for the women's is really long at sporting events or concerts. And there are only two things men aren't supposed to do: pace up and down in hospital waiting rooms smoking Lucky Strikes while our wives deliver babies and hold forth on what it's like to be a woman.

I am not about to violate that second injunction. But the men and women of the Baby Boom are more alike than men and women used to be. I'm trying to imagine my dad acting like my mom. I'm not having much success. And I'm only slightly better at imagining my mom, pipe stem clenched between her teeth, driving too fast with one eye on the road, trying to dial the car radio to a Cleveland Indians game.

The Baby Boom genders are similar, therefore I conclude that the experience of our formative years was similar. The girls were prying up icky things from the busy street of the psyche. They were loading Wham-Os of melodrama with steel ball bearings of emotion. They were lighting firecrackers of hurt feelings, breaking parents' hearts the way we broke parents' windows, and leaving flaming bags of dog poop on the front porch of vulnerable people's sensibilities. And girls were as avid as boys in their attempts to torment a dumb animal, otherwise known as Mom. But, mind you, I was a boy, so I'm only guessing about this.

As well as the facts of life, the fact of death obtruded. Of course, if you came from a large Irish family, somebody was always kicking off. There would be a solemnity to the nagging in getting me into my Sunday school clothes and no baseball game on the car radio. Funeral homes shared their architecture with branch banks. Drive-through deposit windows looked like the porte cochere where the hearse was parked. Why funeral homes were called "homes" was puzzling. And a strong smell of cut flowers in any kind of home was as surprising then as the smell of boiling cabbage and tobacco smoke would be in a home today. Other than that the atmosphere, full of grim faces and dull carpet, was reminiscent of a visit to a larger and more populated principal's office. Up at one end was a dimly remembered kin of Dad's, partly scary, partly waxy, and partly covered by the horizontal Dutch door of the casket. A weeping aunt would say, "The good die young." I'd wonder what she was talking about. He was in his forties.

But these deaths were adult matters. Sonny Merton was our age. He lived several blocks away, a sinewy, freckled, and unpleasant boy. He'd grab you by your wrists and yell, "Do you know why they call me Sonny?" and shove your fists into your nose if you didn't say, "Because you're so bright." He rode his bike out into the middle of Central Avenue and was run over by an oil truck. For the next few weeks we huddled on the school playground every day before the first bell and talked about nothing else.

Mostly we discussed how squashed Sonny had gotten. Several kids claimed to have special knowledge of the accident. "I heard the siren when the ambulance came." "My dad talked to somebody who lives right near Central." "I saw a oil truck downtown that I bet was the same one." According to the evidence of this testimony, Sonny had gotten very squashed.

We all said, "There's no one like Sonny." We all said, "Gosh, that Sonny!" We all said we'd known Sonny well. A few kids, who had, went to his funeral and were objects of envy. "They had to use rubber and stuff to make him look human again but then they wouldn't let us look at his body anyway."

It was the most interesting thing that happened all year. And now, when I listen to myself and my friends rue distant violence among hostile peoples or possible extinction of man-eating sharks or thawing ruination of inhospitable arctic wastelands, I confess that sometimes—not always, but sometimes—I hear an echo of Sonny's name from the school playground.

*   *   *

We weren't soft kids. We aren't a soft generation. We couldn't be or we wouldn't keep getting our own way. And we've been doing so for more than sixty years. Our parents called us soft because we didn't get up at 4 a.m. to help Pa drag a mop through the dust bowl or wear underpants made of barrel staves because Ma couldn't afford burlap or work two jobs to put ourselves through grade school or squat in the basement all night with a piece of cheese in our hand because mousetraps were too expensive.

We kids were called soft because we didn't go through what our parents went through, which they were usually lying about. And now we call kids soft—their flabby fingers plopping out text messages, bodies barely capable of enough wiggle for Wii, mounds of suet parked in front of LED screens with body mass indexes to make Jerry Harris look like Olga Korbut. I say that and then I go outside and see kids on skateboards and funny little bicycles and snowboards and twin-tip skis doing things that would have scared the worst word I knew out of me in 1959.

There's no such thing as soft kids, at least not in their hard little hearts. I admire the way modern children are trying to break their necks, but I also worry about them. They wear helmets and knee pads and wrist braces. Every post and pole they slam into is padded. The piles of wood chips beneath their slides and swings are as deep as the curbside autumn leaf piles that no one's allowed to burn anymore for fear of harmful air pollution. The rubber mats under their monkey bars are more cushy than what their moms use for yoga. And skate parks, ski hill terrain features, and indoor climbing walls have been built with care to make youthful high jinks harmless.

You'll never get to be a splendid generation like the Baby Boom doing harmless things. Run, kids! Flee! Go ride your boards and bikes down the handicapped access ramps with which every building in America has been so inclusively and sensitively equipped. Nobody's using them anyway. They're too steep and treacherous to be ascended in a wheelchair, except by Paralympic medalists. (And you may become one.) Or, better yet, get the Uncle Walter that I had.

He was not one of those happy-go-lucky younger uncles like Uncle Timmy whose antics had to be discussed out of children's hearing. Uncle Walter was a respectable uncle, a vice president of something in a corporation and graying at the temples. We celebrated the Fourth of July at his cottage on the lake.

The summer after I turned eleven Uncle Walter gave me a grocery bag filled with fireworks of every type and kind. Then he handed me a lit cigarette. Not to smoke, of course—the 1950s were a different time, not a different planet—but because this was considered a sensible way for children to ignite fireworks. Playing with matches was dangerous.

I and my like-equipped cousins were turned loose on the beach. Fourth of July taught the Baby Boom an important lesson (albeit one we've frequently ignored). It's a given that the stuff of life will blow up in your face, just try not to set it all off at once.

If I could go through it all again,
The slender iron rungs of growing up,
I would be as young as any.
                    —Robert Lowell, "Realities"

6

ENDS AND MEANS

Then one day childhood was over, darn it.

Youth, of course, would last forever. The infinite prospect of being young stretched to a horizon that no member of the Baby Boom has reached yet, unless we're dead. But it takes a lot of growing up to stay permanently youthful, so we put away childish things.

Or we claimed that someone put away childish things for us. Billy and Bobby Stumf were going on a scenic picnic with my family. Such was our region of the Midwest that the limestone outcroppings at the local state park were considered scenery. One particular rock formation also made a credible scale model of Iwo Jima. There was a crag to represent Mount Suribachi; two flat stone shelves for the

Japanese airfields Motoyama No. 1 and Motoyama No. 2; loose gravel mounds where the fierce battle of the "Meat Grinder" took place; and a little crevice to use as the cave where General Kuribayshi would hold out until the bitter end and, to our delight, commit hara-kari. All around was a sea of grass controlled by the U.S. Navy. (Billy and Bobby and I had been there before.)

The Baby Boom would become the Generation of Current Events—highly aware, highly informed, highly involved. But like many Baby Boom characteristics this was self-generated. It didn't come naturally. If you'd asked my young friends and me about the U-2 spy plane flown by Francis Gary Powers being shot down over Russia or Adolf Eichmann's capture in Argentina or rioting in the Belgian Congo, we would have regarded them as hazy events of the distant present. But we knew everything about Iwo Jima.

I suggested to Billy and Bobby that we bring our cigar boxes full of lead soldiers on the picnic. "No," said Billy, who had attained the dignity of eighth grade. "Our dad says we're too old to play with soldiers."

And so was I.

Mr. Stumf—he of the machine-gun noises and the dead Jap money in the attic—carved miniature fighter planes out of balsa wood in his spare time. He built a train layout that consumed the Stumf basement, barely leaving Mrs. Stumf room to squeeze between the freight yard sidings and the Maytag. Fifty years later it occurs to me that Mr. Stumf would have been the last person on earth to tell his sons they were too old to play with soldiers. It was Billy and Bobby who had gotten to the point where they used the train layout mainly for train wrecks involving their sister's dolls—and not so often anymore even for that.

*   *   *

Then there was the day when my new pair of Keds didn't fit into the diamond-shaped openings in chain-link fence the way my outgrown pair of Keds had. Chain-link fence seemed designed to accommodate children's feet. And childhood was hemmed around with chain-link fence.

The neighborhood had a few short spans of pickets or palings or split rails, randomly located for decoration and keeping nothing in or out. When the Greatest Generation really meant to fence a place they used chain link. Nice people strung it upside down, with sharp twist-tie points on the ground and smooth folded ends in the air so kids wouldn't rip themselves to shreds. Less nice people did the opposite. We scrambled up and over regardless. For twelve years it had been a shame to use a gate. And now my foot was stuck. What if girls were watching?

We'd quit not noticing girls, not that we noticed much. We were blinded by the dazzling thought that, under their clothes, they were naked. So we still didn't know what they were doing. I asked my wife, "What were girls doing when they were thirteen?"

"We were spying on the boys," she said. "We'd get together and say, 'Let's go spy on the boys.'"

I was afraid of that. And me looking like an idiot with my foot stuck in the chain-link fence.

Looking like idiots may be why we stopped jumping off airing decks. That and the fact that our growing weight meant we had to find and drag home at least three discarded mattresses to break the fall. And we were too big to fit down clothes chutes. What if somebody found out about *that* at school, how Mom had called the fire department to pull on my ankles because I was butt-stuck with my legs flapping above the laundry hamper?

What ever happened to clothes chutes and to those second-floor decks at the back of the house where the dust mop was shaken and the bedclothes were aired? They were once such common features in the Midwest. Modern houses are full of conveniences—climate control, WiFi, home entertainment centers, indoor gas grills, elliptical exercise machines, and custom-built walk-in wine cellars. But what do you drop the cat down? And where do you heave water balloons from?

But I wander from the subject. And because the subject is the coming of age of a large portion of the American public, all of whom have been through that, maybe it's just as well. I'm certainly not going to talk about sexual awakening, especially not my own. The human heart, with all its mystery, wisdom, and inspiration, is worthy of endless exposition. The human penis is another matter. Let's just say that, like childhood, it was hard to let go of.

The Baby Boom faced a difficulty in leaving childhood behind. We had no motive to do so. Our fathers weren't household tyrants. They weren't even home that often. All the domineering patriarch sob stories of the past—from Abraham's insistence on a career path that was all wrong for Isaac to King Lear's overcompensation for his inability to express affection to Cordelia—could have been resolved by the introduction of golf. And our moms were "understanding." They'd read Dr. Spock, women's magazines, and newspaper advice columnists. Maybe they couldn't bring themselves to discuss sex in detail but, in general, you couldn't shut them up about "the changes young people are going through."

My mother took me aside and solemnly informed me, "If you ask a girl to go swimming, and she says she doesn't want to, don't insist. Not even if it's a sunny day and she's in her bathing suit and you're right by the water. She may have personal, private reasons for not wanting to." I was baffled. And I remained baffled for several years, until my high school girlfriend—that great reader of information on feminine hygiene product packaging—explained the problem and how it could be fixed with a switch to tampons.

Our understanding moms were more useful when we sneered, pouted, had snits, and went around slamming doors. Then Mom would start in on "the changes young people are going through" and Dad would go play golf instead of grounding us.

We didn't feel cramped by the limited, provincial circumstances of our upbringing. We'd get to that. Circumstances seemed okay at the time and were going to get lots better when we were old enough to drive. Our parents told us they'd given us everything. An obvious untruth because where was the moped, the .22 rifle, the aboveground backyard pool, and the pony? But they told us so often that we half believed them. We had it good at home. Subsequent generations figured this out, which is why they're thirty-eight and living in their mom's basement.

We were eager to move on. It's a phrase we're still fond of using, even now when what we're moving on to is assisted living. We wanted to be older, greater children—cooler kids—and we were willing to make the necessary sacrifices.

Instead of jumping off airing decks we went to a flooded quarry where there was a cliff called "Suicide." It was as high as a church steeple or, anyway, as high as a phone pole. And girls could see you. (Although some of them didn't want to go swimming.) I spent most of a junior high summer day nerving myself to jump off Suicide. But I took a wrong lesson in graceful descent from circus trapeze artists leaping into their nets. I held my arms straight out at my sides. Palms, posterior forearms, triceps, and armpits got spanked bright red on the water. I spent the rest of the afternoon flapping my elbows as if playing Flying Horses—looking like an idiot.

We endured private lessons. These were not as ubiquitous as they would become, but the intent to give children "advantages" and "accomplishments" was the same. Not that our parents had any idea what advantage we'd gain by having these accomplishments or how our accomplishments were supposed to be an advantage. "Condoleezza Rice would make a great secretary of state, but can she figure skate and play the piano?"

Music was the most frequent of the lesson crazes our parents went through. Billy Stumf had a trumpet and was very good at getting spit to dribble out of the spit valve, and he could make extraordinary farting noises with the detached mouthpiece. Steve Penske produced haunted house ghost groans on a Hammond organ. Johnny MacKay sang in the church choir. He was so embarrassed by his boy soprano that he practiced hymns at home with a voice like the wrong frog being kissed by a princess. Susie Inwood was learning the violin, and Jerry Harris, who lived directly across the street, had taken up drums with special emphasis on the cymbals. Between the squeal of one instrument and the crash of the other it was as if our block were having an all-day car wreck. Nobody's parents objected much when we abandoned music lessons.

We also abandoned petty vandalism—in favor of petty crime. We slipped a comic book inside another comic book and paid the cashier for one comic book instead of two. We pocketed Dad's change from the top of the dresser. We swiped cigarettes from Mom's purse. We rummaged around at the back of the liquor cabinet among the less frequented bottles of things such as Chartreuse and took a putrid sip. In these misdemeanors we were led by Joe Brody, one of those kids who are real trouble that we met playing sports. Joe would go so far as to take the family car when his parents were asleep. But he only took it around the block.

Come to think of it, we weren't there and had nothing but Joe's word to go on that he really did this. As a generation we were always more law defying than lawbreaking. Our parents, with their greater experience of callous authority, were law evading. Especially around April 15 and on the highway—"Help Daddy watch for speed traps." When the Baby Boom was finally apprehended by the police, it happened at protests and demonstrations. We would be arrested as a matter of principle. And/or drugs.

Not that we completely gave up vandalism. (To judge by what I hear about the state of politics and the economy and marriage and the family and the flaming bag of dog poop that we left on the front porch of Iraq, we never did.) We'd just learned how to t.p. a house. The trick is to be tall and strong enough to throw an unraveling roll of toilet paper all the way over the roof.

Prank phone calls weren't immature. Our parents and their friends made prank phone calls at parties, if everybody had had enough to drink.

"Let's call the NAACP and tell them that knock-knock joke . . ."

"Who's there?"

"Eisenhower."

"Eisenhower who?"

"I'se in Howard Johnson's, eatin' lunch!"

The Greatest Generation was not at its best on racial issues. And a receding conscience seemed to us to be a normal part of growing up. Unlike a receding hairline. We've spent millions to stem that tide. Our conscience had been slipping away for a while. It was years since any of us had yelled, "I'm telling!" And it would slip further. The Baby Boom is a moral generation but not necessarily a conscientious one. A byword of our twenties and thirties was that nothing—not commercial white bread, not refined sugar—was as unhealthy as guilt. And we turned out to be a healthy bunch.

We'd started with a conscience. When I was just old enough to be allowed to go around the block on my tricycle, I pedaled up the driveway of Mrs. Furstein, who was arty. Behind her garden shed she had a pile of the kind of rocks, brought from the seashore, that were considered artistic when arranged in a garden. I climbed the chain-link fence around the shed, boosted a rock over the smooth folded ends of the fence top, put the rock on the back step of my tricycle, and pedaled up the driveway of Mr. Biedermeyer. Then, fulfilling some mission of the imagination that I can't recall, I hid the rock in Mr. Biedermeyer's two-car garage, behind the boat. I did this twice and was wracked by guilt.

Bitter self-reproach kept me awake whole halves of hours past my bedtime. One night I finally got up, went down to the kitchen in my pajamas, faced my mother, and told her everything.

Purloined Furstein rocks smuggled to the Biedermeyer garage makes no sense, and it must have made even less sense when recounted by a four-year-old. But Mom said the right thing, "I'm sure you didn't mean to." And I didn't mean to do all the things I did in the 1960s and '70s either.

Nonetheless we are, as I said, a moral generation. When the little qualms of guilt that we'd shooed off at the end of childhood and kept shooing away through youth and early adulthood came back to us at last, they'd grown huge. Mrs. Furstein's artistic garden rock is as big as the planet and we will experience catastrophic species extinction if we don't get it out of the atmospheric concentration of greenhouse gases in Mr. Biedermeyer's garage. But my feelings about my first wife are still healthy.

Getting finished with childhood wasn't wholly unpleasant. We were on probation from the Garden of Eden, not expelled. We'd eaten only a tiny bit of the fruit of the tree of the knowledge of good and evil, and we'd spit out most of it. So our eyes were only half opened. For example, women were only half naked even with their clothes off, as we found out thanks to Joe Brody's stepfather's subscription to *Playboy*. The Baby Boom girls certainly weren't in sorrow bringing forth children. Not at fourteen. Not in those days. None of us had gotten as far as under-the-sweater-over-the-bra or even Spin the Bottle. The ground wasn't cursed for our sake except when we had yard work chores. We didn't eat the herb of the field. Mom had given up trying to make us finish our vegetables. Nor did we, in the sweat of our face, eat bread. We spent our allowance on Peter Paul Mounds bars, Fizzies, and Pez candy in plastic novelty dispensers.

We had a day pass to get by the cherubims at Eden's gate. And if we were nimble we could avoid the flaming sword of adult intervention in our new liberties, new interests, and new friends. I took the bus downtown to the main library. I needed to look up things for my report on "America's Greatest Inventor," who was Henry Ford. Or maybe Thomas Edison. Possibly it was Alexander Graham Bell. Those three guys and the Wright brothers had invented everything. I should have written down which one I was supposed to do the report on. I'd look it up in the main library's huge encyclopedia. Should I pick the *A* volume for "America's Greatest Inventor" or the *G* volume for "Greatest Inventor" or the *I* volume for "Inventor"? Or should I get off the bus one stop early and meet Joe Brody at the bowling alley?

Steve Penske got his ham radio license. Ham radio was invented by the Wright brothers, I informed him. It took Steve six months to learn Morse code. Johnny MacKay and I memorized a little for use in classroom desk tapping. You can guess what *dit-dit-dah-dit dit-dit-dah dah-dit-dah-dit dah-dit-dah* spells.

Steve kept his shortwave radio in the attic. The wire antenna was strung along the rafters. We'd watch while the radio tubes warmed up, then Steve would broadcast to the world.

"Calling any station. Calling any station. Calling any station. This is W8QRX."

And sometimes, faintly, with a lot of crackling, someone in a distant place such as New Jersey would reply, "W8QRX this is W2EFZ."

And a conversation would ensue.

"W2EFZ this is W8QRX. Do you read me? Over."

"W8QRX this is W2EFZ. Roger. Do you read me? Over."

And so on, in case you thought Twitter was newly moronic.

Johnny MacKay bred guinea pigs. They eat their young. This does not turn out to be a conversation starter with girls at YMCA dances.

I customized plastic model cars. Plastic model cars were not toys like plastic model airplanes. I cleared the plastic model airplanes out of my bedroom in case someday, eventually, I got a girl in there. Building plastic model cars was a design exercise. My design inspiration was Futurism. Future being when I turned sixteen. Then I'd have a car. Meanwhile, in 1:24 scale, I worked on the shape and form this car would take. (Although when I finally got a car of my own I did not, in fact, glue an airplane wing to its trunk lid.)

There was a fad for building model cars. It is claimed that the Baby Boom youth was a period of great faddishness due to the growing powers of savvy on Madison Avenue and television mass marketing—coonskin caps, Frisbees, hula hoops, Pez dispensers. And this faddishness, in turn, is claimed to signify something about the Baby Boom. Perhaps. Faddishness seems a constant in human affairs—phone booth stuffing, "Killroy Was Here," flagpole sitting, muttonchop sideburns. The fad for dying of tuberculosis may have signified something about the Victorian Age. Ascribe significance to the hula hoop, you who can.

Billy and Bobby Stumf devoted themselves anew to sports. Both were stars of our junior high football team though Billy would be demoted to the second-string freshmen squad at the immense local high school and relegated to playing loose end or way, way back. Billy and Bobby wore their football uniforms while carrying their football helmets under their arms more often than the demands of games or practices or the duration of football season required.

Jerry Harris collected rocks. All boys collect things, and most boys collect most things—baseball cards, birds' nests, cigar bands, bottle caps, matchbook covers, arrowheads (or pointy stones that might be arrowheads). Once junior high school maturity strikes, a self-respecting boy may continue collecting but only if his collection is overorganized, obsessed upon, analyzed, and labeled. And he has to hold forth about his collection. That is, a boy who collects baseball cards must be able to make even other boys who collect baseball cards squirm in tedium with numbing details about why Washington Senators third baseman Harmon Killebrew's card from 1959, when he returned to the majors and played in the All-Star game, is a real prize. Jerry Harris wasn't good at holding forth. Nor was he much of a geologist. He labeled all the rocks in his rock collection "limestone."

I collected comic books, not all of them pilfered. I inherited Susie Inwood's collection when she began dating. The superhero comics were frankly dull. Their authors and artists ran afoul of the same problem Billy, Bobby, Johnny, Steve, Jerry, and I had had trying to play Superman. The superheroes were so more powerful than a locomotive, so faster than a speeding bullet, so busy pulling gizmos out of Robin's tights that they made short work of ordinary miscreants. Preposterous villains had to be created to give the heroes a fair chance to not win.

There was a censorious fuss about comic books, started by the psychiatrist Fredric Wertham's 1954 book *Seduction of the Innocent,* which maintained that horrible, gory, and violent comic books were bad for us kids. A thoroughly incompetent shrink, Dr. Wertham had not delved into the horrible, gory, violent minds of kids. But he had a point about comic books being bad for us. From Lex Luthor, Mister Mxyzptlk, Bizarro, the Joker, the Riddler, and the Penguin, the Baby Boom got the idea that evil is weird and alien. Hannah Arendt's idea that evil is banal is almost as bad, but more banal.

Human sins of greed, pride, envy, sloth, and wildly sputtering wrath were better elucidated by Donald Duck in the comic books written and drawn by Carl Barks. At the age I was, I wouldn't have dared to be seen with a Donald Duck comic book, but hidden in my closet I probably had the complete works—Huey, Dewey, Louie, Gyro Gearloose, Gladstone Gander, and Scrooge McDuck, in mint condition. If Mom hadn't cleaned out my room after I went to college I'd be too rich to be writing.

Grown men had collections. President Franklin D. Roosevelt famously collected stamps. I, with a stamp collection of my own, thought he'd had an unfair advantage. The White House probably gets a lot of mail. My godfather went through his pocket change every evening, looking for buffalo nickels, Indian head pennies, and the steel one-cent pieces that were minted during World War II. Uncle Timmy had a collection of miniature liquor bottles that were, amazingly, considering Uncle Timmy, still sealed and full.

It was the age of hobbies. Mr. Stumf was still working on his train layout. This was beginning to cause conflict with his sons. He kept trying to sneak down the basement to install flashing lights at Lionel grade crossings when he was supposed to be drying the dishes. Meanwhile Billy and Bobby kept trying to sneak down the basement and extract swiped copies of Joe Brody's stepfather's *Playboys* from concealment under the train layout when they were supposed to be doing their homework.

Mr. Harris raised fancy guppies—English Lace, Spanish Dancer, Blue-Tailed Tuxedo. They eat their young too. But since Mr. Harris was not, presumably, in need of conversation starters with Mrs. Harris, it wasn't as shocking.

Most dads and granddads had home workshops where they . . . where they preferred to be left alone. Periodically a bulbous table lamp turned on a wood lathe would emerge or a fretwork knickknack shelf fresh from the jigsaw. Mom would hang the shelf or place the lamp and there the item remained for a certain length of time. Afterward it could be found in the attic. My paternal grandfather made things out of pipe and pipe fittings—a banister, a railing around his yard, the legs for a card table. Grandma was dead so these stayed put.

Hobbies are less common now. Or, like our little guilts, they've grown huge. We turn our hobbies into passions. You start with an ordinary five-thousand-bottle collection of Grand Crus in the custom-built walk-in wine cellar and the next thing you know you own a vineyard. Follow your passion. And not just any vineyard but a vineyard in a place where no one has ever thought to make wine such as the Amazon rain forest.

Hobbies are private things. Passions demand to be conveyed. We are not a private generation. Our hobbies make great TV—"Rain of Terroir." Mr. Harris's guppies would not make great TV. Or maybe I'm wrong. "Tomorrow on *Mr. Harris, Fish Hoarder*, 'They Eat Their Young.'"

But Mr. Harris was too self-conscious to be on television. And we're too self-conscious not to be. Self-consciousness is our salient trait. This would be on full display in a few years, when we were raising consciousness—of ourselves—and achieving a higher level of consciousness—of ourselves. In the meantime we self-consciously quit riding our bicycles.

We'd just gotten new bikes. We'd saved every grand-parental birthday and Christmas five-dollar bill (and Dad's change from the top of the dresser), pushed lawn mowers for crabby old people, done odd jobs like tearing down the MacKay garage, and pedaled around paper routes on our antique balloon-tire Schwinns with big, dumb wire baskets attached to their cow horn handlebars. Or, doing even harder work, we'd wheedled our moms and dads. Finally we got what we called an "English racing bicycle" (nowadays called "a bicycle") with cool skinny tires, neat drop-down handle-bars, no basket, nifty hand brakes, and three gears.

But when the summer after eighth grade was over we put our English racing bicycles in the garage. And we left them there. A high school student couldn't ride a bicycle, any more than a high school student could be dropped off by his mother right in front of the place where he was going. She had to stop and let him out blocks away. We'd walk. (Joe Brody hitchhiked.)

That summer I was on another scenic picnic with my fam-ily at the state park with the limestone outcroppings. The park also had broad fields of mown grass like a golf course but without Dad yelling, "Watch the hell what you're doing, you'll get hit by a golf ball!" I was running across one of these fields, just running for the heck of it, utterly thoughtless. Or not quite utterly. Because I remember thinking was this maybe the last time I would ever just run for the heck of it?

And, sure enough, when I started high school there was President Kennedy's President's Council on Youth Fitness, taking the fun out of running.

Not all that tempts your wandering eyes
And heedless hearts, is lawful prize.
—Thomas Gray,
"Ode on the Death of a Favourite Cat,
Drowned in a Tub of Gold Fishes"

7

ALL THAT GLISTERS

Mr. Biedermeyer, who took a walk around the block every evening before dinner, began wearing Bermuda shorts and knee socks. It was a new era. Things were changing.

For a long time nothing had happened in the world. At least, nothing much that the Baby Boom noticed. The launching of Sputnik had caught our attention and caused a brief flurry of interest in science and math until we discovered this meant more dividing fractions. Billy Stumf's dog's name on an artillery shell was my strongest impression of the Korean War.

Nothing may explain a lot about the Baby Boom. Ike was the president. Khrushchev was the dictator. Pius was the pope. In December 1959 *Life* produced a special edition, "The Fabulous Fifties," and I thought, "What?"

We'd been living in a steady state universe. Meanwhile grown-ups had been experiencing—at the speed of light—big bangs, red shifts, black holes, and general theories of relativity. Old people had gone from a world with the noise of horses' hooves in the street to a world where the noise was Elvis.

Only we, who had been born after 1945, knew that life was stable, fixed, reliable, safe. And boring. So the Baby Boom has always believed passionately in change. What's the harm in it?

So far, being a freshman in high school didn't seem like real change except, JFK or no JFK, I was on my own fifty-mile hike because I was too self-conscious to ride my bicycle. The nation may have entered upon the sunlit uplands of the American century, but a fourteen-year-old doesn't have an *age d'or*, especially if they've got you taking French.

School had become a little more confusing. High school teachers couldn't seem to leave it at teaching. They talked a lot. Miss Benton the French teacher talked about the significance of French nuclear weapons in Charles de Gaulle's *Force de Frappe*. (She'd been to France, the summer after she got out of college.) "Power of milk shake"? The *Beginning with French* textbook didn't have much in the way of a glossary.

Mr. Keeble the History teacher said, "America has a vigorous young president." The president was in his forties. His wife gave a televised tour of the White House full of all the old furniture you could shake a stick at.

Miss Benton dressed like Jackie Kennedy and tried to talk like her, to the extent that a strong midwestern accent allowed. (What did *that* sound like in French?) Miss Benton wore pillbox hats, oversized sunglasses, pointy shoes, and skirts that ended a little closer than skirts usually did to teacher knees. She had a huge rear end.

Mr. Keeble could get into a heated debate, mostly with himself, about Quemoy, Matsu, the Bay of Pigs, and Laos. He wanted us to ask questions. And we had some. The *Ohio, America, and the World* textbook didn't have much in the way of maps.

The first lady sounded like she was talking baby talk. Marilyn Monroe talked baby talk too. What was it with important adults talking baby talk and urging us to talk like adults about important things such as the Cold War, counterinsurgency, and the Green Berets? But if I raised my hand to ask whether it was, maybe, kind of embarrassing to make our toughest, most lethal military unit wear *Force de Frappe* things on their heads, Mr. Keeble smirked.

Then he caught himself. Teachers were supposed to "engage" us. Education in the 1960s couldn't seem to leave it at educating. Engagement with students was the first step education took as it meandered off toward "relevance." Education was changing.

It worked. The Baby Boom has engaged in all sorts of things. And we consider ourselves so relevant to the world that we think we can stop rising sea levels by separating the glass from the plastic in our trash.

But it's difficult, in retrospect, to say what penetrated the mind of a high school freshman. I don't recall having much mind, and what I did have wandered.

Mr. Keeble went on at length about the New Frontier. It lacked Comanches, gunfighters, and cattle stampedes but had the Peace Corps. I couldn't picture myself dramatically wounded and bleeding to death while bravely urging Sargent Shriver to leave me behind and repair the village well.

What did impress itself on the nascent 1960s adolescent brain was all the talk that things were changing. Things like soldiers and Girl Scouts wearing the same berets? We could do better than that. The seed of the Baby Boom's you-ain't-seen-nothing-yet was planted.

And the growth of boredom was nurtured. It had sprouted in first grade and now began to bear fruit and has done so ever since. Ask Baby Boomers to explain the most dramatic episodes in our ever transforming opinions, attitudes, careers, marriages, and ways of life and we'll tell you—when we're feeling honest—"I got bored."

Algebra was very boring. "There are some things you don't want to know" is not a Baby Boom phrase. We're a knowing generation. Nonetheless, if such things did exist, I suspected that what $\frac{x}{\sqrt{y}}$ equals was one of them.

Mr. Wiley the Algebra teacher was old. Engagement with students probably sounded to him like some kind of violation of the Mann Act. Education did not meander for Mr. Wiley. We'd have to look at the *Mad* magazine we had tucked inside the *Algebra Now* textbook if we wanted relevance.

There was a future irony awaiting us in the Algebra class boredom. The Baby Boom's billionaires are the kids with dandruff, smudged eyeglasses, unmatched socks, and misbuttoned shirts who joined Math Club freshman year and now commute by helicopter from Greenwich and Palo Alto where they live with their Generation Y smoking hot third wives. Software algorithms and formulae for finance market mathematical models (damn you, Mr. Keeble, for never mentioning them) explain why ironic vies with easily bored as the typical Baby Boom frame of mind.

I was bored by my old friends. I had nothing in common with them now. Billy Stumf was on the West Side High JV football team, although he was still second string, so he could say hello to me in the halls. Bobby Stumf was in eighth grade. Steve Penske was becoming "hoody"—slicking his hair, turning up his jacket collar, and smoking cigarettes closer to the school entrance than was allowed. Johnny MacKay had moved and went to North Side High. He rooted for the North Side Polar Bears instead of the West Side Cowboys.

We're a mobile generation. Or, as Johnny MacKay put it, "Why didn't Dad move us to *California*?" The Baby Boom would expand American geographical and social mobility. Americans used to head outward and upward. We'd beat that. We'd head downward and backward too. Downward all the way to the hollers of Appalachia, as the folk music mania was about to prove, and backward to the tenement slums about which our grandparents had kept us ignorant. (So ignorant that in my hipster twenties when I moved to Greenwich Village and saw my first rat, I left a bowl of water out for it because I thought the kid next door had lost his pet.) Our identities themselves are mobile, like our biker gangs of fellow retired business executives. Frequent change of friends is necessary. Though eventually we go on Facebook and get back in touch. "Hey, what you been doing since Miss Burbage sent you to the principal?"

Joe Brody was in my homeroom. The half hour before lunch was occupied by Homeroom, the purpose of which was unclear. Attendance was taken. This meant you could have skipped the first half of the school day—as Joe Brody found out, while the rest of us lacked the courage to act on his findings. Important announcements were made over the school PA system by someone using broadcast equipment borrowed from Steve Penske's ham radio set. Our generation has certain shortcomings. I blame the school PA system. Probably the important announcement was "All students reporting to Room 110 at three p.m. will be given a dose of common sense."

Ana Klein was also in my homeroom. She saved a place for me in the high school cafeteria. Not that there was a crowd trying to sit with the freshmen, although there might have been if Ana hadn't worn her hair in a Martha Graham bun and walked like a duck the way girls who take too many dance classes do.

Ana's cousin Tim Minsky sat with us. He didn't have dandruff or wear glasses or need help buttoning his shirt. He hated being smart in math. He knew what $\frac{x}{\sqrt{y}}$ equals.

"So tell me," I said.

"There are some things you don't want to know."

Leo Luhan thought he was cool. He sat with us because we, and only we, thought so too. Joe Brody sat with us because the other kids who were in as much trouble as Joe had skipped the rest of the school day.

Jim Fisk was too thoughtful to sit anywhere else. He was practicing to get on the debate team. We listened to "Resolved: The United States Should Not Sell Wheat to the Soviet Union Because a Soviet Union Wheat Surplus Will

Be Used to Build Nuclear Warheads." In return Jim listened to physics equations that proved high school doesn't exist, why the Kingston Trio would change American music forever, tales from detention, how Martha Graham's contribution to modern dance had transformed *West Side Story*, and concerns about Green Beret headgear.

And Al Bartz was too thoughtless to sit anywhere else. He was funny. He could fart at will.

Of course I had nothing in common with my new friends either. That was different. Jerry Harris farted a lot. But not at will.

What I could do at will, and even more so when I willed otherwise, was get erections. Perhaps something needs to be said about the human penis after all. I would get an erection hurrying from class to class between bells so that I'd have to carry my books like a girl. Carrying my books like a girl provoked enough thought of girls to give me another erection in class. Then I would be called on to stand up and give an answer about the independence of emerging African nations and why it was like the New Frontier.

If it weren't for the protective spread of open three-ring binders propped on desktops there would be no adult male Baby Boomers. We all would have died of embarrassment.

I'd get an erection at the family dinner table and have to carefully dawdle over my lima beans for reasons other than *Kukla, Fran and Ollie*. I'd get an erection at Uncle Walter's cottage when my older cousin Shirley wore a two-piece bathing suit that revealed her navel. I'd have to stand around in water up to my waist for no reason while Uncle Timmy accused me of peeing in the lake. I always had an erection in the morning. Someone should have taken my mother aside and solemnly informed her, "If you ask a boy to get out of bed, and he says he doesn't want to, don't insist. Not even if he's late for school. He may have personal, private reasons for not wanting to."

Our turgid toy fox terrier Pee Wee had died—just when I was beginning to sympathize with his plight. But Pee Wee wanted to hump everything. The indicator of my desire, like a compass needle (apt simile for a hundred-pound, five-foot-two-inch boy who spent half an hour every night examining legs, underarms, and groin in hope of a dark hair), swung around to the magnetic north of sophomore Marsha Matthiessen, in the frozen terrain of the hopeless crush.

If self-consciousness is the salient trait of the Baby Boom, the crush is the signal emotion. Our generation is not given to tragic passion—too tragic. Nor are we much for stolid affection that matures and strengthens with age. (March 1, 2012, item from the *New York Times*: "Over the past 20 years, the divorce rate among baby boomers has surged by more than 50 per cent.") The perfect love is the crush—*Romeo and Juliet* without the plot resolution. What's the harm in it?

We're an expansive generation. We would discover that we could have a dozen crushes at once, while even three or four simultaneous affairs led to complications. Nor did our crushes need to be limited to persons. We could fall for groups of people—social classes, ethnicities, races. In a few years we'd show up wearing bell-bottoms, work shirts, Stetsons, braids, clunky turquoise jewelry, and sandals. Smitten by various exotic types, we'd imitate the dress of sailors, ditchdiggers, cowboys, Indians, Mexican peasants, and Jesus all in one outfit.

We'd get crushes on moods. Groovy. We'd get crushes on slogans. Make love not war. (Fortunately we got over that one before we had to apply it to Osama bin Laden.) We'd get crushes on abstract ideas. The Whole Earth. And we still do. The balanced budget. We'd have passions for diseases. Everybody had mono, then it was chronic fatigue syndrome, now it's Asperger's. And all our children are allergic to peanuts.

Philosophies, politics, and religions have been the objects of our unrequited love. From Jean-Paul Sartre we'd find out what's up with *Being and Nothingness*. (Nothing, as far as I could tell from the book.) The "liberal consensus" meant "You won't have Nixon to kick around anymore." (He was fibbing.) And it turns out the Maharishi Mahesh Yogi smiles like that at everybody. We would feel unrequited love for love itself. All you need is unrequited love. And our crushes would last as long as we cared to let them. Love never dies when what you love doesn't know you're alive.

However, in 1961 I was a beginner with crushes. Marsha Matthiessen was a slight girl, almost elfin. A full-sized homecoming queen would have been aiming too high even for the permanently elevated angle of my imagination. Besides, Marsha Matthiessen had wonderful qualities all her own.

She lived ten blocks from me, and at night I'd walk in drizzle or slush or biting cold to observe those qualities. That is, to observe the lighted windows of the house in which those qualities were displayed.

Inside, at the Matthiessen dinner table, Marsha was giving her opinion about selling wheat to the Soviet Union and what $\frac{x}{\sqrt{y}}$ should equal. She was laughing at how Al Bartz had commandeered the school PA system and announced that Federal Communications Commission chairman Newton N. Minow's speech to the school assembly about "The Vast Wasteland" had been canceled due to a scheduling conflict with *Wagon Train*. But she didn't laugh at Leo Luhan for bumping into a drinking fountain because he was wearing sunglasses indoors, being cool. She liked modern dance but not enough to walk like a duck. If she had a chance she'd let Joe Brody drive her dad's Corvette. That was her dad's Corvette, the one parked near her house sometimes. I was sure of it.

In the blue television glow behind the living room curtains, Mr. and Mrs. Matthiessen were watching reruns of Jackie Kennedy's White House tour. They'd say I was too young for Marsha, and too wild at heart. Marsha was bored by old furniture. The light on upstairs, that was her in her bedroom, flipping through a fashion magazine with an eye to getting the U.S. Special Forces into uniforms of the latest style. And she was fantasizing about having sex with someone less hairy than a sophomore or a junior or a senior boy. In every imaginable position. I knew of three. Sometimes there was a light on in the basement, where the workshop would be. Marsha harbored a secret fondness for customizing plastic model cars.

I never said anything about my crush. Al Bartz would have made some wisecrack, called her "Bluie, the M&M that's not in the pack." I did mention her name to Billy Stumf (I mean, you can't not *ever* speak of the eternal love of your life). Billy was a sophomore and maybe knew . . . "Yeah," Billy said, "melts in your mouth, not in your hand!"

I had nothing in common with my old friends now, but we did that nothing together most weekends. Billy was out for the season with a ruptured spleen. Bobby Stumf was still in eighth grade, but he was bigger than any of the rest of us. Johnny MacKay didn't like North Side High. Steve Penske was having trouble being hoody. He was expected to pick on littler kids, and there weren't many kids who were littler, except me, and he'd already suffered the effects of my roundhouse right. Unfiltered cigarettes made him sneeze. He liked menthols, which were for girls. And it turns out ham radio is not hoody. Jerry Harris was still in eighth grade too, but Mr. Harris didn't notice if we got into the Chartreuse or even the Baileys Irish Cream. We could do anything we wanted in the Harris basement as long as we didn't smoke near the guppies.

When Joe Brody came over we planned to make trouble like we used to. But we seemed to have lost the knack. Sometimes we'd go to where roadwork was being done on Central Avenue and rearrange the traffic cones so that drivers found themselves in a lane too narrow to pass through.

Joe had an idea for a prank on Johnny's high school. The Polar Bears' homecoming game was next week. They'd be playing the Cowboys. We'd get a ton of weed killer and write BEARS BITE on the football field grass, which would get brown and dead just in time for the game. We didn't have enough money for a ton of weed killer, but Mr. Biedermeyer was a fanatic about his lawn and he'd have lots in his garage.

We'd catch Joe's stepdad at just the right moment, a six-pack into being good-natured, and tell him a story about donating weed killer to a poor family on the north side of town who couldn't afford to take care of their yard. He'd put the seven of us in his car, with the weed killer in the trunk, and drop us off behind the Polar Bears' stadium. We'd wait until late at night and scale the chain-link fence. (Note how, later, the aging Baby Boom—having never forgotten our youthful dreams and aspirations—would equip everyplace with surveillance cameras as soon as they were invented.) And we'd work by match light and Zippo flame until past midnight spreading weed killer in big block letters. But Mr. Biedermeyer's garage was locked.

I told Ana Klein all about Marsha Matthiessen. Girls understand these things. Ana asked me if I wanted to see *West Side Story*. Her parents balked at going for the fourth time. Taking Ana to see *West Side Story* was not, per se, a date. It was a mutual attendance at a cultural event.

As with television, tail fins, the suburbs, fads, and JFK, movies are supposed to have had a profound influence on the Baby Boom. And maybe they did. At the end of a good 1960s movie the characters died. Especially if they were the characters that the Baby Boom audience liked. Not just in *West Side Story* but in *The Alamo, Spartacus, To Kill a Mockingbird, Bonnie and Clyde,* and *Butch Cassidy and the Sundance Kid.* At the end of *Dr. Strangelove* everybody dies. This taught the Baby Boom a lesson. In marketing. If our generation had been running the movie industry when *Dr. Strangelove* was in production, Stanley Kubrick would have been fired and replaced with Todd Phillips and Slim Pickens would have ridden his H-bomb into a Mai Tai being drunk by Zach Galifianakis where it would have fizzled and *Dr. Strangelove* would be a franchise with Part VIII coming soon in 3-D to a multiplex near you.

As I was saying, taking Ana to see *West Side Story* was not a date. Ana and I never dated. But we experienced the painful logistics of early teenage dating. My mother drove.

If my mother and Ana and I all sat in the front seat we'd look ridiculous. If I sat in the back, Ana would be exposed to inquiries from my understanding mother. My mother had taken dance classes when she was a girl. She and Ana might have a conversation. And if I sat in the front and Ana sat in the back, my mother would drag me into the conversation, doubling the embarrassment.

Baby Boom parents were picking up on ideas from Mr. Keeble and other adults. Mom would try to engage us. The whole adult world was failing to keep its distance. The generation gap was a hope long before it was a catchphrase.

Ana and I both sat in the back. I insisted that we be dropped off three blocks from the movie theater.

I didn't get *West Side Story*. The west side was the good part of town. (Although parts of the north side were nice too.) Prevailing winds blew factory smoke to the smelly east side. The teenagers, who seemed to be going on thirty, were supposed to be hoods. But they were singing songs and dancing like Ana Klein. And the Jets wore gym shoes. Steve Penske would never wear gym shoes. Hoody kids wore black, pointy shoes from Thom McAn.

We were reading *Romeo and Juliet* in freshman English. Mrs. Orpington the English teacher said *West Side Story* was *Romeo and Juliet* retold. But the Montagues and Capulets were both Italians like the Jets were, although none of the

Jet families seemed to own Italian restaurants, and the Sharks were from Puerto Rico and talked like Speedy Gonzales.

Tony and Maria on a fire escape was sort of the same as the balcony scene in Act II, but they were on a fire escape, so it was sort of the same as a *Mad* magazine parody of the balcony scene in Act II. And what kind of name was "Jets" for a teenage gang? Over in Cleveland there was a teenage gang called the Vice Joys. That was more like it.

If Romeo and Juliet hadn't kept going on and on about whether it's larks or whether it's nightingales they would have had time to do it again in Act III before Lady Capulet started hollering. Then they die.

Mr. Keeble talked about *West Side Story* and *Romeo and Juliet* too. The underlying issues were relevant to the poverty problems in America today, and the resulting conflict was relevant to the Katanga rebellion. "If the United Nations charter had been in force in Verona the UN would have intervened with the Capulets and Montagues the way Dag Hammarskjöld intervened in the Congo," Mr. Keeble said. Dag Hammarskjöld died.

At the end of *West Side Story* Maria doesn't die. At least I think she doesn't. By that time Ana Klein was in tears and I was in mystification. I put my arm around Ana and said, "There, there," because that's what men said to women who are crying, as opposed to what boys said to girls who are crying, which is, "Knock it off."

When the movie was over my mother was waiting in the car right outside instead of three blocks away. I pulled my arm free and looked at Ana and said, "Knock it off."

Years would pass before I realized Ana Klein was cute. And she liked me. For a knowing generation, we got off to a slow start.

Myself when young did eagerly frequent
Doctor and Saint, and heard great Argument
About it and about: but evermore
Came out by the same Door wherein I went.
                    —Edward FitzGerald,
                        The Rubaiyat of Omar Khayyam

8

AGENTS OF INFLUENCE

Adolescence is a time of discovery. The Baby Boom discovered beer.

At about the same time we discovered beer we discovered that, now we were older, our parents went out at night. We never wondered where they went. Possibly the Greatest Generation had a social life. To us it seemed unlikely. We were the center of the universe and if our parents weren't orbiting close by then they were out in the void of space where events that didn't immediately concern us took place.

Meanwhile we also discovered that Jim Fisk, with the serious expression on his face, looked almost old enough to buy beer. Not that the clerk at Lefty's Package Goods paid much attention to a customer's appearance as long as he appeared to be tall enough to reach the counter with $1.10 for a six-pack of Blatz. We'd go over to somebody's house that night. His parents were out.

Beer was the miracle multivitamin of Baby Boom male adolescence. The necessary requirements for our generational growth were provided in large doses. Beer gave us the confidence to deal with our salient trait of self-consciousness. Beer quelled our reserve about divulging the secrets of our signal emotion the crush. Beer made us brave, cheerful, and sick all over the kitchen floor. The effects of beer were extraordinary. What else could have made a teenage boy mop the kitchen?

Then Mom and Dad come home and the place still reeks of beer and vomit. Mom goes upstairs, not being understanding for once, which is a relief, and making loud sighing noises. And Dad sits you down for the first man-to-man talk since the sex one. It's a rite of passage.

"I guess this is what they call a rite of passage," Dad says.

Without beer—and assuming the reader was as bad at being a loudmouthed obnoxious high school sports star as I was—what would there be for a Greatest Generation dad to take a certain sneaking pride in?

Beer has been good to the Baby Boom. Our greatest achievement has been in the field of communications. We were just then developing our first form of new media—the instant, high-speed dissemination of our ideas and opinions for which the Baby Boom is famous. And mooning people never would have occurred to us if it hadn't been for beer.

One of our ideas and opinions is that inhibitions are unhealthy. Inhibitions are almost as unhealthy as guilt. Beer is health food. We wished we could get the girls to partake more. We wished we could come up with a special beer for girls. It's a problem. What is beer for Baby Boom girls?

Sometimes, of course, it was beer. Although the girls got more silly than uninhibited. They made it to the bathroom before they threw up. And they never made it with us. We're supposed to be a generation with a short attention span, but we worked on the beer-for-girls problem for twenty years. Mateus Rose? Wine coolers? Pot? LSD? As it turns out, cocaine was beer for Baby Boom girls. Cocaine is not health food. Alas.

Another Baby Boom idea is that we know everything. And now we do, thanks to the Internet. But we already had the secret to learning what's what. You can click on an icon or you can pull on a pop top. Information is one beer away.

Al Bartz informed us that the Blatz brewery was started by a distant relative of his but that the Japanese immigrants in Milwaukee couldn't pronounce Bartz because, phonetically, the letter L is almost the same as the letter R except that L is an alveolar lateral while R is an alveolar glide.

Al had done a paper on phonetics for extra credit in AP English titled, "Why the Japanese Say, 'Rots of Ruck.'"

The Baby Boom's greatest achievement of all has been in the field of bullshit. We excel not merely at communicating but at marketing, public relations, political campaigning, high finance, law, the oracular sciences, everything to do with the World Wide Web, and all professions that employ important-sounding jargon.

Yet another Baby Boom idea is that life is like high school. We are the first generation to make this claim. It's hard to imagine the GIs of D-day standing around on Omaha Beach saying, "Life is like high school." Life was not like high school in ancient times. Although a prom date with Henry VIII could turn out to have a *Carrie* ending. Nowhere in the philosophy of Plato does the phrase "Life is like Plato's Symposium" appear. But if you consider the role that bullshit plays in the modern world, life is like high school.

I mean *bullshit* as no insult. The Greatest Generation created the atomic bomb. The Baby Boom created the story that Saddam Hussein had one. (Please do not answer the question "Which was worse, Hiroshima or the George W. Bush administration?" if you've voted for Dick Gregory, John Anderson, Lyndon LaRouche, Ross Perot, or Ron Paul. Especially don't answer it if you've voted for all five.)

Our generation is identified with drugs. Use of drugs has declined. Because we took them all. But it was beer that revealed our true qualities. And memo to Generation X with your microbreweries and your hops and malt snobs: beer is quantitative. Speaking of which, our parents drank more than we do. Why wasn't alcohol the path to success for them? Probably it had something to do with their guilt and inhibitions. I'll have to ask Al Bartz. He became a psychiatrist.

Using our talent as communicators, we communicated the Baby Boom idea that we are each perfectly unique by acting in complete unison with a clique (which we pronounced "click") of six or eight other kids who we thought were just like us. That way the one-of-a-kind nature of our self was multiplied by six or eight—enough to make an impact on life, which is like high school.

In the high school of the early Baby Boom everyone dressed the same. This was how we communicated our idea that we were nonconformists. Identical clothing demonstrated the individualism of the Baby Boom. Tim Minsky, being good at math, explained it after two beers. The theory of quantum mechanics predicts that infinite random behavior results in universal laws of physics.

The universal law at our high school was boys wore penny loafers with white wool socks, chinos, and long-sleeved madras shirts. Individualism was expressed when the madras bled on Dad's white dress shirts.

Girls wore penny loafers, too, with white cotton ankle socks, pleated tartan skirts, and Peter Pan collar blouses embellished with circle pins. Boys told each other that a circle pin meant a girl was a virgin. Whether it was meant to mean that or not, it did.

This style was known as "collegiate." Any college would do, even the two-year college downtown. Kids who were going to work instead of college didn't need to communicate nonconformity and could wear anything they liked. Except blue jeans.

The school authorities forbade work clothes in school. However, the school authorities said we had to work hard in school. Otherwise, when we left school, we'd have to do hard work. Probably wearing blue jeans. "Question Authority," as the aging dork in a Prius who held me up in traffic this morning said on his bumper sticker.

Questions of legal, moral, and institutional authority began to be fiercely debated in public schools. The fierce debate of the 1962–63 school year was whether white Levi's were blue jeans.

Today the question of whether students should be given condoms is fiercely debated in public schools. Speaking as someone who carried around the same Trojan until it wore a white ring in the leather of my wallet, it's amazing how much bullshit our generation has piled on legal, moral, and institutional authority. The fierce debate of the 1963–64 school year would be whether students should be given haircuts.

Anyway, were white Levi's blue jeans? The school authorities maintained they were Levi's. The students maintained they were white. Parents and teachers got involved. Jim Fisk's debate team adviser changed the debate topic from selling wheat to Russia to "Resolved: White Levi's Are Not Appropriate Apparel for School."

We're a generation that doesn't back down on matters of principle. Starting in 1963 boys at our high school wore penny loafers with white wool socks, white Levi's, and long-sleeved madras shirts.

White Levi's weren't the only pressing issue of the day. Mr. Collingwood the Biology teacher interrupted class during the Cuban missile crisis. He told us that this was a very grave crisis. There was a genuine threat of nuclear war. We should have a class discussion.

My Biology lab partner, Susan, was no Marsha Matthiessen but she was cute enough that I'd dissected her frog for her.

I told Susan, "We could be dead next week. You and I should, you know, do it."

Susan gave me a look like she'd given the frog when it came out of the jar of formaldehyde.

"No, seriously," I said. "We don't want to die virgins."

Susan gave me a different look, more like the one when I'd pulled her frog over to my side of the table and, shielding her view with my madras-clad elbow, recited the names of frog innards so she could label the diagram in her lab notebook.

She said she needed time to think. She'd give me her answer on Monday. Then the Cuban missile crisis was over, darn it.

Pressing issues were becoming popular. Class was interrupted more often. We discussed mutually assured destruction and civil rights. Even parents wanted to have discussions.

Ana Klein's father was a doctor. Her mother volunteered at the city's Planned Parenthood clinic. There was no TV in their living room. They owned hard-back books. They had a poster of Matisse's *La Danse* on the rec room wall and they used cloth napkins on weeknights.

Dr. Klein turned to me at dinner and asked, "What do you think about civil rights?"

Was I supposed to argue? Saying, "Civil rights are great!" didn't sound right either. I had very little experience of any-body talking about anything at the dinner table. I said, "Civil rights are the pressing issue of the day."

Dr. Klein nodded with grave approval. But civil rights were, paradoxically, almost as damaging to the Baby Boom's understanding of the nature of evil as superhero comic books and Hannah Arendt. I hope nobody who was completely right about something that was completely wrong will take offense, but Baby Boomers would end up thinking that each pressing issue of the day—no matter which side of the issue the Baby Boomer is on at the moment—is a matter of, as it were, black and white.

Of course Ana and the rest of us did talk about civil rights and other pressing issues when we were by ourselves.

Dr. and Mrs. Klein went out a lot. They had a wine cellar. That is, they had a cellar with a cupboard that had wine in it. We tried Manischewitz. That makes a real mess on the kitchen floor.

Ana and Leo Luhan were determined to become Freedom Riders. Ana was indignant that West Side High School wasn't integrated. Leo thought the way white people in Mississippi talked, dressed, and acted wasn't cool. They had a plan to be Freedom Riders on the city bus that ran back and forth along Coolidge Avenue between the West Side High school district and the city's black neighborhood. And Joe Brody had a paper bag full of bus token slugs.

But before they could get organized Coach Gurnsey, who coached the West Side Cowboys football team, started worrying that West Side wasn't getting any of the Negro kids who were good at playing football. A former Cowboy football star who sold real estate found a house in the West Side school district for the family of the black neighborhood's best running back. The house was on a street with a lot of new immigrants who didn't speak English well enough to say prejudiced things.

People like Coach Gurnsey and the former football star real estate salesman don't seem to come up in any Ken Burns saga of the American civil rights movement. And I suppose Coach's motives for integrating West Side High wouldn't have made for an elevating classroom discussion about civil rights. But the running back was always called on to explain how it felt to be discriminated against.

Tim Minsky, Jim Fisk, and I signed up for "Model UN." We did it to get excused from gym. At "Model UN" the pressing issue was "Should Communist China Be Admitted?" The answer was no. It would lead to an imbalance for Chinese communists. Later the answer would be yes. It would lead to a balance for Russian communists. Phillip Woo, the only Chinese kid in the city school system that we knew of, did not sign up. His parents owned a Chinese restaurant. Maybe they would have liked 800,000,000 more customers.

"Model UN" was held downtown in the drafty auditorium of the two-year college. There were about a hundred high school student delegates, the kind who want to get excused from gym. I can't remember anything else, and wouldn't if I could. Nothing produces more useless tedium than "Model UN" except the UN.

The Greatest Generation was pretending it was good Cold War strategy to send a bunch of kids someplace to argue about things they didn't understand. In a couple of years the Greatest Generation would quit pretending. In a couple of years the Greatest Generation would really believe it was good Cold War strategy to send a bunch of kids some-place—someplace worse than a drafty auditorium— to do something worse than argue, about things they still didn't understand.

The Baby Boom's greatest achievement has been in the field of bullshit, but we didn't invent it.

No, no; for my virginity,
When I lose that, says Rose, I'll die:
Behind the elms, last night, cried Dick,
Rose, were you not extremely sick?
                              —Matthew Prior,
                                "A True Maid"

9

THE PRELUDE

Bliss was it in that dawn to be alive, but to be young was very heaven, as William Wordsworth said when he got his driver's license.

The Baby Boom's first social movement was cruising. This is not to be confused with "Crusin'"—adolescence on wheels as it is poorly remembered in popular culture and badly reenacted in Plymouth Belvederes by old bald guys. I never saw a carhop wearing roller skates. The idea was as stupid then as it is now.

Nor did we cruise in the singles bar or Chistopher Street sense, loitering with sexual intent. We were full of sexual intentions. And we could loiter. But we had a broader agenda.

We drove around and around. Our parents didn't understand cruising. They thought we were driving around to find a place to drink and make out. Not that we weren't. But the Greatest Generation, with its dull powers of fancy, never suspected that our goal was to have no goal at all. Life is a journey, not a destination, as Ralph Waldo Emerson said when he got his driver's license.

We had the perfect pointless joy of freedom. It wasn't just our parents who didn't understand; neither do we anymore. We as grown-ups tell ourselves as kids (and tell our own kids), "Freedom is a serious responsibility" or, "Freedom means making important choices" or, if we've had a couple of drinks and are listening to an oldies station, "Freedom's just another word for nothing left to lose." We as kids tell ourselves as grown-ups, "No, it's not" and "No, it doesn't." And our kids tell us that Janis Joplin needed Auto-Tune. I leave it to others to decide whether, over the years, the Baby Boom has gained sophistication concerning the ontological question of free will.

We drove around and around. There were a few little red sports cars, hot rods, custom jobs, and bitching sets of wheels. Very few. Turning sixteen caused our parents to break out in a rash of vehicular insipidity. (Any good Baby Boom boy my age can testify that the oomph went out of American family car design in 1963.) Dad bought Mom a snappy convertible back about the time of the Nixon-Kennedy debates. When we got our driver's license, he traded it in on a station wagon.

Only rich kids with indulgent parents and poor kids with after-school jobs had their own cars. And thus began the political trend of Angry Middle-class Resentment. The middle class is furious, or at least as furious as middle-class proprieties allow. You've seen it in the firebrand—well, Weber grill charcoal lighter—demagoguery and the crass rabble-rousing (though we're not rabble, so call it Babbitt-rousing) of recent elections and on *Morning Joe*.

Once the Baby Boom had gone through all its rudimentary phases of ideological development, from revolutionary pimples to Reaganite hip replacement, the true politics of our generation would be revealed. In America the reasonably well-off and moderately comfortable are the angry masses. It has to do with borrowing Mom's car.

Jim Fisk tried seriously to make the best of things. He showed everybody how one pull on a lever caused the whole front seat of his mother's Nash Rambler to fold down into a bed.

Ana Klein said, "You're going to pull the lever and some girl's going to flip over backward and break her neck."

"No girl," said Al Bartz, "is willing to be seen dead in a Nash Rambler."

Turning sixteen caused us to break out in a rash of unwonted helpfulness. "I'll go to the supermarket, Mom. We're almost out of paprika."

We drove around and around. The cars got bad mileage. But gas was 31 cents a gallon. We could get to where all the other kids were by looking under the couch cushions. Unspoken consensus made driving up and down certain streets obligatory and parking in certain places required. Sometimes when we parked we were "parking," as the art of love was called, and sometimes when we parked we were parked. We got out of our cars to talk to each other. We're a talkative generation, and only so much can be shouted from a car window.

We got out of our cars but not away from them. That would have been like separating the body from the soul. Or, not to overstate the case, it would have been like getting too far from a bathroom for the males among us fifty years later. We lounged against the fenders. We perched on the trunk lids. We stood in the open doors with one foot resting on the sill and an elbow cocked on the roof, looking cool. It wasn't just Leo Luhan who thought he was cool. Now we all did. And the cars of those days didn't ruin looking cool with nagging ding-dong noises if you left the car door open and the keys in the ignition.

It's heavy lifting conducting light flirtations. Much effort goes into crafting an effortless guise. We worked up an appetite. Drive-in burger restaurants played a crucial role in cruising. They were parking lots with food.

We had plenty to talk to each other about and plenty of each other to talk to. The Baby Boom was discovering itself—and not in the tiresome way that we would keep doing for the rest of our lives until, by now, every rock in our psyche has been overturned and each wiggling thing we've found underneath has been squashed or made into a pet. Youth was discovering youth. Not only were there lots of us, there were lots more of us. Other kids went to other high schools. The boys were almost as cool. The girls were even cuter.

Driving around was our Facebook. We never thought to monetize it. Generational vice? Or generational virtue?

We drove around and around and we talked and talked. We talked about what's cool and what's uncool. No one listens when teenagers talk, including the teenagers themselves most of the time. But teenagers were (and still are in present-day text messages) having an ancient colloquy of deep significance.

What we discussed appears in the Revised Standard Version of the Bible, Proverbs 17:27, "he who has a cool spirit is a man of understanding." Cool. The *Oxford English Dictionary* cites a line from a Chaucer poem, "thynkist in thyn wit that is ful cole." Spelling bees are uncool. In 1938 Eric Partridge, the twentieth century's preeminent lexicographer of slang, gave a cool definition of *cool* in *A Dictionary of Slang and Unconventional English*: "impertinent, impudent, audacious, especially if in a calm way." This was in common use by the mid-1820s, standard English by the mid-1880s, and exactly what we were talking about by the mid-1960s. In 2010 Partridge's lexicographic heir Jonathon Green, author of the 6,000-page *Green's Dictionary of Slang,* devoted eighteen column inches to *cool* and said, "As with a number of slang's (rare) abstract terms, it is less than simple to draw hard-and-fast lines between the senses."

We've been out of our senses a lot. The Baby Boom was always less than simple. Forget the hard-and-fast lines. We are a fiery generation, heated in our affection, feverish in our action, blistering in our scorn—and obsessed with being cool. Later we'd be a fat generation—obsessed with being fit. We still think we're cool. That isn't all. We still think we're hot.

Good thing we talked this out while we were driving around.

The music we listened to was cool. The power of our generation is our music. But, in the interest of speaking truth to power, I looked at the Billboard Top 100 for the year I went from junior to senior in high school. We liked "Everybody Loves Somebody" by Dean Martin (no. 6) better than we liked the Beatles' "Can't Buy Me Love" (no. 52). We liked "We'll Sing in the Sunshine" by Gale Garnett (no. 8) better than we liked the Kinks' "You Really Got Me" (no. 78). The Rolling Stones didn't make the chart. Leo Luhan had mentioned them. He said you could tell their music was influenced by the Kingsmen's "Louie Louie." Here are the actual lyrics to "Louie Louie" as posted on the Internet, a medium that does not spare our sensibilities.

> *Louie Louie, oh no*
> *Me gotta go*
> *Aye-yi-yi-yi, I said*
> *Louie Louie, oh baby*
> *Me gotta go*

And more of the same. If it's any comfort the previous year's Billboard Top 100 was worse: "Hello Muddah, Hello Faddah, Here I am at Camp Granada . . ." and "Blame It on the Bossa Nova" by Eydie Gorme.

There were three AM stations playing the same songs. This was good because when one station finished playing a song we could push the buttons on the car radio and find the same song being played on another station. We enjoyed hearing songs over and over. As with wearing clothes like everyone else's and belonging to a clique and driving around to the same places at the same times, it forged individual identity.

A lot of identical individual identities were forged. We saw nothing ironic about this. So far the Baby Boom had only a mild, *Playboy* cartoon caption case of the ironic. Irony wouldn't become chronic and severe until the 1970s when we ran out of cool things that we all agreed on and disco happened.

AM radio was the sound track of our life. That was a cool thing that we all agreed on. Leo Luhan considered himself a talented composer of the sound track of his life. He made suggestions to the manager of the drive-in burger restaurant about what should be on the jukebox.

The restaurant had tables and booths inside, where we went when it was too cold to be cool outside. There was a sophomore we knew, driving around with us. He didn't have his driver's license. Leo convinced him to go into the burger restaurant and feed the jukebox so that the right sound track theme song would be playing when Leo walked through the door. Other kids had fed the jukebox. Twenty minutes passed before "Louie Louie" came on. We had to get up on our knees in the restaurant booth and frantically signal to Leo who was waiting in the car and had trouble seeing us through his sunglasses. By the time he got there the jukebox was playing "We'll Sing in the Sunshine."

Everything adults thought we were supposed to do was un-cool. Especially if we were supposed to do it for fun. Adults had a peculiar sense of fun. My wife's book club meets at our house tonight. They're reading a self-help book called *My Life Sucks, I Hate You*. I intend to spend the evening in my basement workshop sorting a coffee can full of screws into small trays according to size and whether they are slotted or Phillips head. Adults retain a peculiar sense of fun.

Homecoming was all sorts of fun. The Homecoming Game was the West Side Cowboys versus their traditional rival the North Side Polar Bears.

"The West Side Cowboys," said Al Bartz, "and the North Side Polar Bears and the East Side Yankees. The school system was really thinking that one through."

At the Homecoming Dance, balloons (sunset orange and buffalo brown, the school colors) were put in the basketball nets. Rented tuxedos made sure the fun was special. No shoes allowed made sure the gym floor wasn't damaged. The chaperones' efforts to curtail lewd personal contact were conducted on principles opposite of today's. Kids pressed together tightly with low lights in slow dances—this was considered sweet. Wild gyrations of the hully gully, the jerk, and the watusi performed four feet from a partner—these were glared at.

Joe Brody had the idea of using a hypodermic needle to inject vodka into a watermelon. Ideas, we were beginning to understand, were important for their own sake. That is, we didn't know where to get a hypodermic needle. Even Joe's parents would miss a whole bottle of vodka. It was November, there weren't any watermelons. And why would anyone bring a watermelon to a homecoming dance? We were almost ready for ideas of peace and love.

The homecoming parade had a float. A flatbed trailer was borrowed from the local plant nursery. Two-by-fours were nailed together to make a framework on the trailer. Chicken wire was bent around the two-by-fours more or less in the shape of a giant, almost-four-foot-tall cowboy boot. "Boot the Bears" was the homecoming theme.

To get a Rose Bowl parade float effect, wads of Kleenex were stuffed into the chicken wire. Kleenex did not make brown or orange Kleenex. The local stationery store donated a roll of brown tissue paper and a roll of orange. BOOT THE BEARS was spelled out in brown and orange on the boot top although with some spacing difficulties so that what parade-goers saw was BOOTT HEB EARS.

I don't remember why I was helping stuff Kleenex into chicken wire. I may have thought, wrongly, that Marsha Matthiessen would be helping stuff Kleenex into chicken wire. I do remember a sudden and strong feeling of being uncool. I am in my middle sixties. I have a teenage daughter. The feeling was stronger than that. The parade float looked like chicken wire with Kleenex stuffed into it.

Ana Klein, by dint of her many dance classes, had been chosen as one of the Tumbleweed Girls. They performed gymnastics on the sidelines at football games dressed alike in western outfits purchased at the local Western Wear store. Al Bartz asked Ana, "Is there a Midwestern Wear store?" She quit.

Tim Minsky ran for student council. His platform was based on a simple formula. Student council had no power. Therefore, if he was elected, he'd do nothing. He won. We'd soon loose our sense of humor about politics. It wouldn't come back until Watergate. When the Baby Boom's sense of humor about politics returned it acted like it had been sleeping in alleys and eating out of garbage cans.

We'd already lost our sense of humor about our parents. If we'd had one. Anything a parent said or did we took personally. (I don't think our children have made this mistake. The lesson in the Baby Boom's lifelong fascination with personhood, personality, and persons is that people shouldn't be taken personally.)

Our parents were generally pathetic. When they were specifically pathetic the pain was intense. Dr. Klein told Ana, Tim Minsky, and me, "I like that Beatles group. Some of the songs those young men sing show that they have genuine musical talent."

"I think they're cute!" said Mrs. Klein.

There was nothing of the remote about our parents. Meaning *remote* as a noun. They couldn't push our buttons from a distance. They had to come right up and try to switch to the channel we were on. They should have stuck with *remote* as an adjective.

We would have detested the twenty-first century's remote-control connectivity—cell phones, texting, twitter. Parents everywhere, like God? (A god that couldn't tell George from Ringo.) The horror is unimaginable to the mid-1960s teenage mind. Parents with a Facebook page. Like a newspaper page but never thrown away. Parents "posting" things, as in a poster, as in a billboard, as in a billboard on a busy street where we were cruising. With things about us on it. With things about our parents. And last summer's snapshots. When I still had a crew cut and my sisters were teasing their hair.

Then we, the Baby Boom, invented electronic personal communication devices. We, of all people. TV that watches you. It's as if we read *Nineteen Eighty-Four*, and said, "Good idea!"

We didn't need connectivity. We were where all the other kids were, cruising West End Avenue, at the drive-in burger restaurant, watching submarine races by the pond in Pondside Park.

The Internet is a universally shared thought process. We had one already. On the first day of senior year Leo

Luhan—with that deliberate flaunting of convention for which the Baby Boom is known—would come to school wearing penny loafers, white Levi's, a madras long-sleeved shirt. And black socks. The rest of us had come to school the same day wearing penny loafers, white Levi's, madras long-sleeved shirts. And black socks.

It wasn't like we hated the grown-ups. Yet. We were capable of real feelings for adults, as long as they had nothing to do with our lives.

In the fall of my junior year John F. Kennedy was shot in Dallas, and in American Literature class. The school PA system —not an electronic personal, or any other kind of, communication device—made the details incomprehensible but the situation clear. There was no mistaking the sober tone and poignant halts in the loudspeaker static for an Al Bartz prank.

Our parents and teachers were shocked because John Kennedy was one of them the way John Lennon was (although, born in 1940, he really wasn't) one of us. That is, they were shocked because John Kennedy was one of them and then some, them more so, them to a greater—and not just presidential—power. Them richer than a king and admirably schooled in every grace.

We were shocked by all the emotion. Embarrassment, crushes, and embarrassment about crushes (and erections) were emotions as we knew them. Most of us had never lost a parent. Most of us had never even lost a parent to a woman younger than Mom. Not being allowed to borrow the car was our understanding of loss. Bereavement was Sonny Merton run over by a truck.

The emotions were so strong that we forgot to be cool. Not that there wasn't something cool about the strength of the emotions and their uninhibited display.

Mr. Entwhistle the American Literature teacher knew a lot of poetry by heart. He began to recite "Richard Cory" by Edwin Arlington Robinson.

> *He was a gentleman from sole to crown,*
> *Clean favored and imperially slim.*
>
> *And he was rich—yes richer than a king—*
> *And admirably schooled in every grace.*

A wildly inappropriate poem, ending,

> *So on we worked, and waited for the light,*
> *And went without the meat, and cursed the bread;*
> *And Richard Cory, one calm summer night,*
> *Went home and put a bullet through his head.*

I think Mr. Entwhistle meant to recite "To an Athlete Dying Young" by A. E. Housman, because he did recite that the next time we were in American Literature class.

> *Now you will not swell the rout*
> *Of lads that wore their honors out,*
> *Runners whom renown outran*
> *And the name died before the man.*

Which we did not exactly understand because West Side High had a trophy case, and everybody who'd won something had his name engraved on a cup or a bowl or the base of a statuette.

But we understood the Kennedy assassination was a significant event for our generation. The significance being that the Kennedy assassination was Pearl Harbor scaled down to the level of the Baby Boom's understanding of actions having consequences.

The consequence of the assassination was only another president, more successful at pushing a legislative agenda—with which Kennedy is wrongly credited—and more effective at pressing a foreign policy—from which Kennedy is wrongly excused. Then myth took hold, in an early 1960s way. *Camelot*, starring Richard Burton and Julie Andrews, had recently closed on Broadway after 873 performances.

> *Don't let it be forgot*
> *That once there was a spot*
> *Where the president was fun*
> *And he's remembered as having something to do with*
> *a drunk actor and a singing nun.*

A generational truth was discovered. How people feel about things is as important as things. Feelings are real. And now so were girls. You could feel them. Eventually. But you had to talk to them about feelings first. (For girls, boys got real too—until talking to us about feelings got unreal at the end of the first marriage.)

I talked about feelings to my high school girlfriend Karen. Although she wasn't my girlfriend yet. She had to be talked into it. I don't mean by me, I mean by the power of talk in general. "They talked themselves into it" is the motto of the Baby Boom. Or maybe "They talked themselves out of it." But we're saving that for our epitaph.

Karen and I talked about feelings in a memorable way. I can't remember any of it. The fragments of our chat that have stuck in my mind for half a century—Karen explaining tampons—can't have been representative of our conversation. They sound more like intimate talk from toward the end of our being a couple, when we were promising to stay together while going to colleges far apart. We weren't talking about tampons in our kiss-on-the-lips-but-no-tongue stage. Nor were we talking about feeling cool and uncool. A boy doesn't speak to a girl about that. To mention being cool to the object of being cool is worse than uncool. It's the quarterback leaving the huddle to join the Tumbleweed Girls. Karen and I just talked. Words are Baby Boom pheromones.

One school night, when I'd borrowed the car and was supposed to be at the library and actually was at the library, Karen and I were sitting across from each other not studying. It was a week or ten days since we'd started talking between classes, in the cafeteria, at the drive-in burger restaurant, on the phone for an hour at a time. I was smiling at her. She was smiling at me. And then I felt an ankle-socked toe just above the vamp of my penny loafer and moving toward the hem of my white Levi's. The erotic shock was so intense that today I am at a loss to explain why I don't have a fetish for toes, ankle socks, or my old left penny loafer.

For a couple of years the Baby Boom was blessed with sure and certain hope. What we hoped for was sex and drugs. Hopes that would come too true but, in our blessed state, not for a little while.

We'd heard about drugs. The marijuana scare preceded the marijuana. We were never able to find any. Leo Luhan and I went to a jazz club downtown and sat through a set by somebody who somebody said sounded something like Charles Mingus. I had no idea a bass fiddle could be as noisy as Susie Inwood's violin. The drug pusher seemed to have had the night off.

However, the fat girl Joe Brody was dating (fat by the ethereal standards of the era and, come to that, we were entering an era where all standards were ethereal) shared her diet pills. Joe stayed up all night writing a paper on *The Scarlet Letter* and the next day, still going, he insisted on reading it aloud in American Literature class, taking up most of the period describing the ways Nathaniel Hawthorne's plot and character development would be transformed if Hester Prynne and Arthur Dimmesdale committed the six other deadly sins, starting with gluttony.

Sex, too, was had in occasional and limited doses. Fumbling anticipation generated a kind of prolonged bliss that fumbled completion has rarely matched. We were tantric when Buddha was still a porker on a shelf over the bar in Phillip Woo's parents' restaurant. No one's life was left in a mess by sex. Although some of our clothing was. What ever happened to the hand job?

It was an existence upon which no improvement could be made except, of course, for elimination of prejudice, poverty, war, and injustice and Dad buying us an Austin-Healey.

We were aware of, if not the nature, the prevalence of evil. "Black humor" was in vogue. There was Lenny Bruce, Paul Krassner's *The Realist*, ice-nine in Kurt Vonnegut's *Cat's*

Cradle, and Al Bartz saying, "How do you unload a truck full of dead babies?"

We were sensitive to grim realities. "*With a pitchfork.*" In our college application essays we pointed out that prejudice, poverty, war, and injustice should be eliminated.

Meanwhile it would also be nice to have a place of our own, a "pad." But who'd iron our madras shirts? (And *not* our white Levi's. "Mom, they aren't *supposed* to have a crease!")

And it would be great if there was no school. But we skipped a lot. Grades don't count after the first semester of senior year. Ana Klein did a good mom voice. "Pat's not feeling too well." We were going to state colleges anyway. Except for Tim Minsky who would be studying math at Yale, to the mystification of most of our parents. "It's so far away," my mother said. "If he went to Ohio State he could come home on weekends."

Perhaps there were as many troubled adolescents then as there are now. But young people are sensitive to fashion trends, and being troubled wasn't in style. Girls weighed ninety pounds and barfed after eating a whole half gallon of butter pecan ice cream. Boys drove cars into phone poles at seventy miles an hour. But anorexia, bulimia, and teenage suicide were unheard of.

We were having fun. The stories we could tell—and do tell and will tell and have told and keep telling in movies, songs, TV shows, memoirs, blogs (though not much in poems and novels—literature is the enemy of fun), and to spouses, children, each other, and to ourself now that we've started talking to that person. There was the time Jim Fisk and I drove overnight to Hell, Michigan, a 422-mile round-trip, so we could say that we'd "been to hell and back." We left right after school on a Wednesday and . . . Oh shut up.

There's proof that it was a wonderful moment for our generation in the very fact of how boring our stories are. Every description of paradise is boring. According to the Bible, Adam and Eve didn't even notice they were naked and spent all day naming animals. It's a shame how the Baby Boom has never learned to appreciate boredom. It would make this current part of our lives more interesting.

Teenage 1960s middle-class America was a shining suburb on a hill. Almost twenty years would go by before we realized that. We've been trying to walk or fly or bum a ride back there since the first John Hughes movie came out.

It wasn't just fun. It was a state of grace. We wanted to bestow our state of grace upon the world. Youth was a virtue. We pitied the moral lapse of those who lacked it. Life was good. We were living. Therefore we were good. Since we were good, and we were mankind, then mankind was good. We'd make mankind as good as itself and living as fun as life. We'd change everything. And we'd write in each other's high school yearbooks, "Don't ever change!"

An' one time a little girl 'ud allus laugh an' grin,
An' make fun of ever' one, an' all her blood-an'-kin;
An' wunst, when they was "company," an' ole folks wuz there,
She mocked 'em an' shocked 'em, an' said she didn't care!
An' thist as she kicked her heels, an' turn't to run an' hide,
They was two great big Black Things a-standin' by her side,
An' they snatched her through the ceilin' 'fore she knowed
        what she's about!
An' the Gobble-uns 'll git you
        Ef you
            Don't
                Watch
                    Out!

                                        —James Whitcomb Riley,
                                            "Little Orphant Annie"

10

THE MAN IS FATHER
TO THE CHILD

Then the decade went to hell.

There was the Vietnam War. We had decided war was wrong. Prominent moralists such as Peter, Paul and Mary agreed. And just when we had decided war was wrong, a war was supposed to be fought by us.

And there was us. Peace violence. Civil rights looting and arson. Protests loud enough to deafen the nation to everything being shouted. Political fantasies so beautiful they made reality get ugly.

And love—like a parody of the verses from I Corinthians 13 that Baby Boomers would later insist be reeled off at each of their weddings. Love paraded itself, love was puffed up, love behaved rudely, love sought its own, love rejoiced in iniquity.

And drugs. Ring-around-a-roach clip. Pocket full of bad trips. Grass, speed, acid. We all fall down. Spinning and giddy, we spoke as children, understood as children, thought as children, and instead of putting away childish things we got put away for them—in jail and mental institutions. Or a few of us did.

It was a day-trip Children's Crusade. We marched upon the Holy Land where we already lived.

(Fun, though.)

A great clash between youth and age began. A generation gap yawned. And so do I.

It never happened. We had parents who were a lot like us. We can tell because they've shown up in the mirror.

We had parents. They brought us up. There's a logical inference that we are products of our birth and upbringing. We are what our parents, consciously or unconsciously, meant us to be. We're the demiurge to their urgency. They were the thought to our deed. It's an irritating supposition.

A supposition the Baby Boom prefers is that we're mutants. "We are the people our parents warned us about." The Jimmy Buffett song was released in 1983, by which time we were indeed the people our parents had warned us about— lawyers, bankers, and politicians.

Some kid somewhere must have been the first to say, "You just don't get it!" Possibly it was Jesus, Gospel of Mark 8:21, "How is it that ye do not understand?" Jesus wasn't technically a kid, but he had the hair and the sandals. What was it that our parents didn't get?

There was the hair and the sandals. But I'm not sure we get those anymore ourselves, even when we're walking around in Tevas with the gray remnants of our mop top tied back in a ponytail.

When I mentioned our parents' "dumpy clothes and vague ideas" I was flattering myself, and the rest of my generation. Look at me in jeans that I'm decades past having the butt to wear or, worse, shorts that everyone under forty wishes it were against the law for Baby Boomers to own. I'm in flip-flops, and not only that it's winter, so I've got on big, floppy socks that the toe thong can squash into. If I have to leave home I'll slip my feet into cushy balloon-sized "athletic" shoes. I'm no athlete. Nor am I quite yet ancient and bunioned enough to be excused for such footwear. And my T-shirt . . . Our parents would not have subjected the scarecrow in their garden to the indignity of old underwear on public display.

If our fathers had been as "dressed down" as we are—which would have meant they were repairing the roof—they'd have been wearing their old military suntans, washed and ironed by our mothers. And our mothers wouldn't have cleaned the oven in what we wear to work. The Avon Lady might call.

As to ideas, the vagueness is ours. What's so funny about peace, love, and understanding? Our parents had a laugh at the Neville Chamberlain peace-in-our-time and the Eddie Fisher/Liz Taylor/Richard Burton lovebirds and the understanding that people are out to screw you. "Confucius say: when rape is inevitable relax and enjoy it." All the cringe comedy of our generation cannot match the shock, offense, and transgressive humor our parents could pack into one old chestnut.

Maybe we're in touch with the "inner dumpiness" of our parents. They were tired of keeping up appearances, longed to let themselves go and be slobs and slatterns. We're doing it for them.

Maybe our parents would have liked a bye on fighting a war. Even Billy and Bobby Stumf's dad wouldn't have minded much. Mrs. Stumf, his high school sweetheart, was a babe. Johnny MacKay's dad and mine and Steve Penske's and Jerry Harris's probably had a stray thought about living it up like Liz and Dick with Mrs. Stumf. Maybe our parents did relax and enjoy a screwing once or twice (or three times, my sisters being twins).

Although, of course, we think, only with each other. The Greatest Generation didn't have our infinite variety of relaxation. The Baby Boom is living the dream.

It seems a little late in life to be coming to grips with this, but our parents were hip. We could make this reassessment on the basis on the Greatest Generation's postures and images —the Rat Pack or even *Mad Men*. But, come on, we had the Greatest Generation around the house. And also tucked under our beds—the "usual gang of idiots" at *Mad* magazine were from the Greatest Generation. The magazine that made fun of our moms and dads was written and drawn by our parents.

Possibly the Greatest Generation had lived a little of the dream themselves. During World War II loose lips may have sunk ships, but loose garter belts were another matter. Our parents were hip to sex. They knew what sex meant. It meant that the number of divorces in America more than doubled between 1941 and 1946—impressive for a generation that stayed married no matter what. The divorce rate of the young Greatest Generation wouldn't be equaled until 1973 when the Baby Boom was old enough to get married, start cheating, and be thrown out of the house.

Our parents were hip to drugs. There was one drug they knew so well that it gave them all the drug know-how they needed. Smoking loco weed was silly drunk. Kicking the gong around was slow-motion drunk. Taking a sleigh ride was drunk and wide awake, ready to drink more. You'd had enough. You needed to keep your wits about you when a bar fight was breaking out between the gobs and the jarheads. You couldn't be sluggish with your up-percut or start goofing on the pretty tinkling noise of all the broken glass when 200 pounds of marine was coming at you swinging a chair.

The Greatest Generation knew how to handle their li-quor. My uncle Timmy said, "At lunch, have gin. When you go back to the office you want people to think you're drunk, not stupid."

And they were hip to rock and roll. Listen to Count Basie, Benny Goodman, Glenn Miller, Dizzy Gillespie, Lena Horne. Now listen to the Kinks' "You Really Got Me." We're the squares.

Our parents were conformists. The Greatest Generation knew camouflage as a technique, not as an ironic fabric pattern. They liked to blend in. We like to stand out. They might have told us a little more about the quantitative versus qualitative ways of being noticed.

I had a summer job in college, working construction, and showed up at the site tonsured and clad as one was in the 1960s. The grizzled foreman watched me fecklessly hammer and saw and, glancing from my Rapunzel hair to my bell-bottoms, said, "You know something, you don't need to *look* like an idiot."

There are some other things the Greatest Generation might have told us—and probably did while we weren't paying attention. (Our generations are well matched in this respect. They spoke their wisdom rarely, we listened to it the same way.) The trophy elk doesn't hang around in the Elk Lodge parking lot during hunting season. Our generation doesn't hunt elk much. We're trophy elk preening on the Hartford Insurance Company rock wearing a Target logo T-shirt.

Our parents were joiners, belonging to every kind of organization, association, and fraternal order. We claim to have been blackballed from Sam's Club. They were wise to safety in numbers. Life is a high-wire act. They weren't going to work without a net. We network. And some interesting bounces we've taken.

We can't believe they were serious about their meetings, rituals, bylaws, and rules of order. They weren't. The veterans' organizations got serious on Memorial Day. During the other 364 (and that night after the Memorial Day parade) the American Legion post and the VFW hall were places to get drunk. We think Shriners in fezzes driving miniature cars in circles is ridiculous. It was supposed to be ridiculous. We believe we have fun. They had more fun. Anybody who's having fun at an Elk Lodge meeting has the fun thing figured out.

Our parents were hypocrites. No matter what they were up to they tried to look and act like they were doing the right thing. They didn't exactly pride themselves on their hypocrisy, but they were proud of knowing right from wrong, and being a hypocrite showed you could tell the difference.

"Hypocrite" is one of the Baby Boom's strongest terms of disparagement. We're as proud as our parents of knowing right from wrong (and think our knowledge is superior). But when we're wrong, we get to show off. We lead a life of modern luxury, and nothing is more luxuriously modern than indulging in the egotistical pleasure of personal honesty about misdeeds. In the California King–sized bed of the ego, on the four-hundred-thread-count sheets of pleasure, we like the honest embrace of vice better than the sanctimonious pillow talk of virtue.

(Although we're quick enough to jump out of the sack, lock vice in the en suite bath, slap on some lip service, run a brush through our sophistry, and wrap ourselves in floor-length false piety if one of our kids shows up without warning.)

(And let's not confuse personal honesty with anything we do at work or on the Internet.)

Our parents were Philistines, comfortably conventional in their views. I don't mean to disparage our parents. I admire the Philistines. Archaeologists tell us that the Philistines were a prosperous Bronze Age society that excelled at the production—and consumption—of alcoholic beverages. They have my sympathy in the Bible. First there's Samson busting their chops and raising the roof because he had to get a haircut. Then comes little David, annoying the Philistines with his slingshot and his nutty music—"a cunning player on an harp." And the next thing you know he's king of the heap. Samson and David seem like harbingers of the Baby Boom.

Our parents put effort into philistinism. It was getting harder to remain comfortably conventional in your views. Psychology and sociology were explaining that nothing is really your fault, and neuroscience was gearing up to prove

it. Henry Wallace's Progressive Party and Joe McCarthy's Sen-
ate hearings were muddying the waters in Stalin's well of
pure evil and Ike's fountain of perfect good. The Theory of
Relativity meant . . . What did it mean? One guess was that
everything's relative. In-laws included? Modern literature and
modern art were sending the message that what had always
been right was left. Left, that is, to the interpretation of the
individual. "My kid could paint that" was our parents' interpretation. (But, though tens of thousands of Baby Boomers
would major in the Fine Arts, the Picassos among us have
been thin on the ground.)

We think of ourselves as skeptical about organized religion.
Even when we're religious what the Baby Boom prefers
is loosely organized, large, new, denominationally vague
churches out in the suburbs where they've just found Jesus.
My sister goes to one.

"I found Jesus," my sister announced.

"Were you," her twin asked, "playing hide-and-seek?"

If Jesus had squeezed under the bottom shelf of the linen
closet in the house where we grew up and crawled behind
the stack of old bath towels He might have won.

We think of our parents as conventionally religious.
We're half right. They were conventional. But I don't remember any adult talking about religion outside church.
Not even the church's pastor, not even right outside church
on the church steps greeting the congregation after church,
when you'd think the subject might have come up in passing.

I presume that the want, the war, and the murder of
the twentieth century left our parents with some questions
about God being a nice guy. But with the resolve the Greatest

Generation so often showed they resolved not to think about it. Or so I presume. They weren't talking.

They went through the motions and maintained the forms. They taught us our bedtime prayer—almost word for word from the seventeenth-century Puritans—without thinking about the thing being frightful.

> *Now I lay me down to sleep,*
> *I pray the Lord my soul to keep,*
> *If I die before I wake,*
> *I pray the Lord my soul to take.*

The MacKays, with their hellfire/sand wasp/bicycle-chicken-in-the-parking-lot church, went most Sundays. The Penskes and Harrises went to their church less often. My parents rarely went to church but sent my sisters and me to Sunday school. There was a private service on Sunday mornings, with the kids out of the house, the neighborhood quiet, and the stores closed. That was when the Greatest Generation screwed.

The Stumfs went to various different churches. Billy said, "My parents are shopping for a church." I have a mental image of Mr. and Mrs. Stumf pushing a shopping cart down aisles lined with Christs, Yahwehs, Allahs, Buddhas, Shivas, Gaias, and Indian totem poles—Baby Boom spirituality *avant la lettre*.

Johnny MacKay received adult baptism by total immersion at the YMCA pool his church had borrowed for the occasion. Johnny said, "We're wearing these white gowns, and after the girls got baptized and the gowns were all wet and they climbed out of the swimming pool, you could see everything they've got!"

Joe Brody was Jewish, at least on his mother's side. At his bar mitzvah the Reform synagogue looked like every other church except the stained-glass windows were abstract art and there weren't any crosses. (Christian symbolism would be problematic if Jesus had been condemned to death more recently. The noose might work. But the electric chair? The gas chamber? The lethal injection gurney?)

Later I'd be invited to a Passover seder with the Kleins and the Minskys at Ana's house. The Minskys were theoretically Orthodox but could never remember which knives and forks were the dairy utensils and which were the meat utensils when their more orthodox Orthodox relatives visited from Cleveland. The Kleins went to temple on Yom Kippur.

"Why is this night different from all other nights?"

"No bacon," said Tim.

When I began Methodist confirmation classes, pondering the nature of God became an absorbing interest along with building plastic car models and trying to kill squirrels with my slingshot.

I felt I had to have a serious talk with my mother. I told her, "I was baptized Presbyterian. Dad's family is Lutheran. I went to Methodist Sunday school. The theology [a word I'd just learned] is really different. Presbyterians believe in predestination [an even better word I'd just learned]. Lutherans believe in salvation only through grace. And Methodists believe in grace, good works, and free will."

My mother said, "It's the church where all the nice people in the neighborhood go." She was reverent in her faith. And, fifty years later, so am I. I believe she's in the heaven where all the nice people in the neighborhood go.

*   *   *

Our generation is not prejudiced. But neither were our parents. They didn't prejudge races, religions, ethnic groups, gays, or women in the workplace. That would have meant they'd made some kind of judgment, that they'd thought about it. They hadn't. The Greatest Generation took the world as it came. People who looked different, talked different, and acted different were different. The hell with them. People who were the same were enough trouble. Negroes didn't get a good education, couldn't get a decent job, and were looked down upon by society. And likewise for the brother-in-law.

The Greatest Generation didn't care for being around people who were different. We love it. (Or we're sure we would love it. One of the Baby Boom's few secrets—guilty or otherwise—is that when we actually met African Americans, Hispanics, and Muslims, and they turned out to be the same as us, we were disappointed.) We embrace people who are different. Nonsmokers only, please.

To say the Greatest Generation "took the world as it came" isn't to say they were passive. An awful lot of the world came right at them, armed and angry and filled with woe. They could handle it.

The Greatest Generation integrated the armed forces and Little Rock Central High, passed the Civil Rights Act, sent their daughters to law school, and founded the gay liberation movement by watching Liberace on TV. Our gripe with them is that they did the right thing without being enthusiastic about it. Why couldn't they be more like the Baby Boom is with recycling and proudly celebrate time spent in the trash bin of human behavior separating vice from virtue?

My family wasn't bigoted—by the standards of the day. Although my grandmother remained convinced until she died in the 1970s that "pickaninny" was a term of endearment. She would use it out loud to compliment moms on their toddlers at the grocery store.

My mother thought prejudice was funny, a good attitude —by the standards of the day. When I was in high school she confided that her sister Margie's husband, Murray LeVine, was actually Jewish, not French, like Aunt Margie said he was. Uncle Murray and Aunt Margie lived in a tony suburb where the tennis club was restricted. If Uncle Murray was French, so is Mel Brooks.

The tennis club excluded not only Jews but Catholics, which sheds more light on why I'm Protestant than Granddad's annulment story. In the Greatest Generation, if you couldn't pass as a white Protestant, you acted like one. People applauded your effort to blend in. The Three Stooges were Jewish. Passing was multiculturalism—by the standards of the day.

When I was three or four, I was riding in a car with my godfather. He was cut off in traffic by another driver, who was black. "Damn zigaboo!" my godfather said. A few days later I was riding in a car with my father. I pointed out the window and said, "Damn zigaboo!" After I'd been scolded and questioned my father went to my godfather and blew up. To judge by the number of times my godparents told me the story, and by the way they mixed admiration with amusement about this rare outburst from "a real gentleman," Dad had strong opinions on the subject.

My father had been in the Philippines with a navy construction battalion in 1944 and 1945. After he died I found a photo album in our attic. There were snapshots of him and a young lady. Palm trees could be seen in the background. The young lady was very like my mother in size and shape and even smile but much darker. It may have been an innocent friendship. But if my father received a horizontal education in the higher moral principles, I'm sure he was enthusiastic about it.

But our parents were repressed. We are not. We're convinced on these two points. Then we learn all about John F. Kennedy. We consider JFK. We consider the photos I found in the attic. We consider our fathers. And we're the ones repressing that thought.

But we're uninhibited. Our parents were otherwise. Although my mother told me she fell in love with my father while they were dancing on a table in a nightclub. My father would get divorced from his first wife in 1946.

My godmother, with the extra First Amendment rights of a nonagenarian, tells me that three kids and a decade later my dad was asleep in his chair, newspaper in lap and highball on end table, when my mother decided to add spice to their marriage. Mom took off all her clothes, put on a raincoat, crept through the back door, went around to the front, and rang the doorbell. Dad stayed asleep. Then Mom discovered she'd locked herself out. She threw pebbles at my window until I woke, came downstairs, and opened the door. Dad slept through it all. And I—thanks to repression—don't remember a thing. But if I did I'd be putting it in a memoir. The Baby Boom is uninhibited.

* * *

But . . . But . . . But . . . Politics. Politically, the Greatest Generation and the Baby Boom were diametrically opposed in the 1960s. Our parents were so conservative, especially when they were liberal, like Dr. and Mrs. Klein who, every time they agreed with us about eliminating prejudice, poverty, war, and injustice, began by saying, "If Adlai Stevenson had been elected . . ." They were reacting, the reactionaries. We were the action. We were the act.

And yet consider a statistic from 1963, before Baby Boom activism had been activated, when the Civil Rights March on Washington had just happened, the Berkeley Free Speech movement was still limbering its tongue, and the first major protest against the war in Vietnam was a year away. In 1963 the federal income tax rate on the head of a household who was making $300,000 a year was 91 percent. The Greatest Generation were better pinko radicals than we would ever be, by one measure.

If the Greatest Generation and the Baby Boom are so closely akin in our ideas and our attitudes, then why all the 1960s screaming dinner table arguments? It was a noisy decade, but the screech of electric guitar feedback, the chants of "Ho, Ho, Ho Chi Minh!," the shots of National Guard rifles, and the wail of police and ambulance sirens were all drowned out by parents and children shouting at each other across the pot roast.

We were arguing with ourself. And we weren't making much sense.

NIXON IS A FASCIST PIG!
GET A HAIRCUT!

Well, who among us has not had a screaming, senseless argument with ourself about actually having done what we actually wanted to do?

I ATE THE WHOLE HALF GALLON OF BUTTER PECAN ICE CREAM! *I'M A FOOL!* I STARTED SMOKING AGAIN! *I AM SUCH A JERK!* I BOUGHT A BOAT WITH THE KID'S 529 COLLEGE FUND! *I'M A SHITHEAD!* I GOT DRUNK AND E-MAILED SMUT TO THAT HOTTIE GRAPHIC DE-SIGNER AT WORK! *I AM A WORTHLESS ASSHOLE!*

And so another decade goes to hell.

. . . whose strenuous tongue can burst Joy's grape . . .
　　　　　—John Keats,
　　　　　　"Ode on Melancholy"

11

THE GREAT DISCONNECT

But this is America. We go to hell in a cheerful, optimistic, can-do American way.

Jim Fisk and I were enrolled at Mediocre State University, and on our first day there Jim exclaimed, "We can do anything!"

He was reading the MSU course catalogue. Registration began the next morning. I looked at the variety of classes available and at the requirements to graduate with a major in one thing or another. "English" caught my eye. I speak that.

We were already smoking cigarettes, drinking coffee, and wearing blue jeans in a school cafeteria. "*College*," said Jim—a heartfelt sentiment that reverberates to this day, echoing in our hearts down through all the decades since.

MSU in 1965 was still college as college was supposed to be. The traditional scholarly learning, intellectual challenge, fraternal and sororital social grace, BMOC attainment, athletic triumph, and sis-boom-bah rigor were available to Jim and me. But so were lots of other things. The drinking age was eighteen.

The college town was full of bars. Two of them, The Old School Cheer and Final Exam, faced each other across an alley. Each had a patio crowded with students. The guys on the School Cheer patio appeared tall and handsome. Their shirts were ironed and their chino pants were creased. By what means was this accomplished a hundred miles from home? Their haircuts were always just a little past due, in the Bobby Kennedy fashion. How did fashionable guys stay forever one step ahead of the barber? My godfather was a barber. Either you got your hair cut or you didn't.

The guys on the Final Exam patio didn't. Some were tubby. Some were undersized. Many were trying to grow beards. This would be easier than trying to grow tall. They wore wrinkled work shirts and dirty blue jeans. I'd been wearing my same pair since the family had dropped me off at my freshman dorm.

The girls on the School Cheer patio appeared pretty and blonde. Their hair was styled with a cute upturn at the shoulders, a "sorority flip." They filled their sweaters. They wore their skirts a daring inch above the knee.

The girls on the Final Exam patio were maybe not so pretty and blonde. They wore black leotards, denim skirts, and peasant blouses. Their hair was long and very straight. (It wasn't until the next summer at home, when I walked into the laundry room and found one of my sisters apparently trying to commit suicide with a small household appliance, that I realized girls ironed their hair.)

I looked at the girls on the School Cheer patio. I had a vision of a great sexual quest. There would be flirtations and introductions. There would be "chance" encounters at mixers and invitations to dance. Groups of her friends and my friends would get together after the big football game. There would be dates to the movies and dates to romantic movies. We'd probably see *A Patch of Blue* five times. There would be the Homecoming Dance, the Winter Carnival, the Spring Fling, and whatever the heck went on in between—March Hare Bunny Hop, April Showers Raincoat Ball, Mayday Emergency Cotillion. There would be fumbling under clothing in the Kappa Kappa Gamma shrubbery while a house mother tsked out an upstairs window, bestowal of one's fraternity pin or even an engagement ring, and much talk about "our future."

I looked at the girls on the Final Exam patio. They were smoking unfiltered cigarettes and drinking beer straight out of the bottle. I thought, "I'll bet they do it." They did.

When we were home on Christmas break Ana Klein, who was at Selective State University, said, "They've eliminated girls' dorm hours. We can do anything!"

Leo Luhan, who was at Big State University, said, "The secret is to never take a subject you can't bullshit your way out of."

"Music Appreciation," said Ana Klein.

"Poli Sci," said Jim Fisk.

I said, "English."

Tim Minsky said, "Leo is telling the truth."

"But you're at Yale," said Jim, "taking Math."

Tim said, "You'd be surprised."

And these days, when we're beset with the math of statistics, their standard deviations, their sampling distributions, and their blatherskite probabilities and predictions that cause half our news items to begin "New studies show . . ." or "Latest polls indicate . . . ," we are surprised.

And yet, if we'd taken more demanding courses or paid better attention when professors were trying to teach us Math, Statistics, Economics, Demographics, and so forth, we might realize why the Baby Boom has always felt, "We can do anything."

From 1946 until we were done being born in 1964, some 75,821,000 of us made our appearance in previously tidy American homes. At the time the country had about 192 million people. The Baby Boom was almost 40 percent of the population. No wonder when we farted the nation shat.

And even now—after all the heart attacks, cancers, car wrecks, suicides, and fatal slips in the bathtub that the actuarial tables demand—we continue to be one-fourth of the citizenry. We're America's largest minority group ever. And there's been affirmative action. Minority quotas—practically 100 percent of college admissions from 1964 to 1982. Targeted minority recruitment—Selective Service. Reverse discrimination—"Don't trust anyone over thirty!" (U.C. Berkeley political activist Jack Weinberg coined the phrase in 1964. He turned thirty in 1970, and Baby Boomers have been teasing him ever since.) Minority outreach—all those ads for Depends and Levitra on network television. And minority set-asides—Social Security and Medicare.

About 35 percent of the federal budget now goes to those two minority entitlement programs. It's estimated that by

2030, when the last of our generation is struggling with how to get the Depends on after the Levitra's been taken, Boomer-Americans will be raking in Social Security and Medicare benefits costing half of all the money spent in Washington. We're riding down the highway of life in a Welfare Cadillac (with the right-turn indicator blinking for miles and miles). Tax rates will go through the roof. Which should keep those Generation X slackers busy, and maybe take their minds off Kurt Cobain dying.

Besides, our families had money. True, they didn't have much money. In 1947 median family income was $3,031. Median meaning that this was the income for that peculiar family able to look down upon the paltry earnings of exactly one-half of the nation while regarding with envious resentment the other one-half who were rolling in it. Three grand and change is about $31,700 in 2013 dollars. That's only $4,130 a year more than the 2013 poverty threshold for a family of five. In 1947 to be middle income was a blessing of middling proportions.

It was nonetheless a blessing. The Greatest Generation consecrated itself to raising the country's median income, and they would continue with their devotions. By 1964 median household income had reached nearly $49,700 in 2013 dollars, in time to sanctify the Baby Boom with college educations. (Incidentally, don't try this today. Sending an out-of-state kid to U.C. Berkeley, for example, costs $38,000 a year in tuition and fees.)

The growth of prosperity for middle-income Americans is oddly difficult to measure. Like many things government didn't used to be, it didn't used to be a statistical busybody. The Census Bureau has no figures for median household income before 1947. The economist Emmanuel Saez, a professor at Berkeley (which institution seems to keep intruding itself into Baby Boom discussion), has spent much of the past decade trying to determine average income in the United States over the previous century.

Of course income is not the same as household income, especially in a two-income household. And an average is a mean and a mean is not a median. (I told you we should have paid attention in Econ.) Averages are blurry statistics with their ink smeared by champagne spills at the top and damp seeping into empty refrigerator cartons where people are living at the bottom.

Dr. Saez calculates that in the years when the Greatest Generation was growing up—1913 to 1932—average annual income ranged between about $12,000 at its lowest and $17,000 at its highest (2013 dollars). In the years when the Greatest Generation had the Baby Boom at home and underfoot—1946 to 1964—average annual income ranged between about $27,000 and about $45,000 (2013 dollars).

But it's not just the numbers we don't grasp that matter, it's the zigzags on the graph we don't understand that are important too. For the eldest Baby Boom children there weren't any zigzags. From 1946 to 1964 average income climbed the social ladder, with only the merest slips, from shabby genteel to shabby chic. The Greatest Generation had a different childhood. From 1913 to 1932 average income went up, down, way up, way down, and the best year and the worst year were only a couple of years apart. This is why our parents never had any use for shabby—or much understanding of chic.

The economy is a kind of confidence game. Maybe what gave the Baby Boom its confident air is better gauged by gross domestic product per capita—all the money the people in a country make divided by all the people. It tells us nothing about our individual economic circumstance—what we eat—but it tells us a lot about our economic atmosphere— what we breathe.

Adjusted for inflation, per capita GDP for the years 1913 through 1932 averages approximately $8,500. This is the world of our parents. Adjusted for inflation, per capita GDP for the years 1946 through 1964 averages approximately $18,500. This is the world of us. Blood is thicker than water, but gravy is thicker than both. The difference between the manners, mores, behavior, and attitudes of the Greatest Generation and the Baby Boom is $10,000.

However, "We can do anything" leaves us with a lot of choices. An extravagance of choice doesn't necessarily lead to making choices that are extravagantly good. And when we can do anything, the things start to come apart from the doing. Success gets separated from effort. Fame gets separated from merit. Dad gets separated from Mom. Existence has been more confusing for the Baby Boom than it was for the Greatest Generation. Not that we mind. It makes life interesting. We can do confusion.

Jim Fisk was a legacy at Tappa Kegga Brew or I Phelta Thigh or some fraternity, and he considered himself obliged to go to a rush party. His dad had said, "They're a swell bunch of guys," in that Greatest Generation between-us-fellows way—just short of a wink and a nod—indicating there was a bottle of Old Grand-Dad somewhere in the frat house and maybe a dimly lit room where you could go with a date to "neck." It was unlikely that, after twenty-five years, the swell bunch of guys were still hanging around. (This wouldn't happen until later in the Baby Boom years, after *Animal House* was released, the drinking age was raised to twenty-one, and fraternities became cool again.)

When Jim returned to the dorm that night he said, "It's like they were practicing to be adults—all in sport coats and ties."

Perhaps this was a strange objection from a generation that would don an astonishing array of outlandish apparel. But one thing we don't do is wear what we're supposed to wear. With the Baby Boom, clothing's function gets separated from clothing's form. We've conducted life as a costume party.

It's been an important party, which we've needed to attend for serious reasons because we've turned fashions into statements. Army fatigues and old pea coats were a satire on militarism. Work shirts made an ironic comment about work. There's no need to repeat the message 1970s duds were sending. The huge shoulder pads on women in the 1980s were a declaration that women had the power and the prerogatives usually accorded to men, usually in the NFL. Today we wear something comfortable whether we're mall walking or receiving a Nobel Prize because who we really are is expressed by wearing something comfortable, and the king of Sweden should get comfortable with who we really are.

Halloween, you'll notice, has become a holiday for grown-ups. So I take Jim Fisk's point from years ago. Dress as an adult? What a getup.

"If you become a pledge," Jim said, "you have to vacuum the carpet and write term papers for upperclassmen and stand on one leg while reciting the Greek alphabet and they paddle you. After that they're supposed to be your best friends for life. I'm confused about the connection between this and fun."

And I was confused about the connection between actions and consequences in general. Or I was once most of the coeds had prescriptions for the pill. I was also confused about why my literature professor couldn't see the connection between great poets like Bob Dylan and T. S. Eliot. *In the room the women come and go talking of Michelangelo. Something is happening here but you don't know what it is, do you, Mister Jones?* The literary parallels seemed clear to me. Not that I had any use for clarity. That was Robert Frost, greeting card stuff, of no interest whatsoever in the happy confusion of a 1960s dorm room bull session.

Although Frost had an effect on the 1960s. "The Road Not Taken." *I took the one less traveled by, and that has made all the difference.* Then everybody took the road less traveled by, and that made the 1960s.

"Maybe my Anthropology class will explain the significance of initiation ceremonies and fraternities and sport coats," Jim said.

The other difference between the Baby Boom and the Greatest Generation is college. Not that none of them went and all of us did. By 1950, when the GI Bill had done its best work, about 14 percent of Americans had some college experience. But by the time *Animal House* came out in 1978, more than 30 percent of Americans had been at or near a toga party. Anyone who has dealt with an audience knows there's a tipping point when about a third of the crowd gets a joke. E.g., in the "Where Are They Now" clips at the end of *Animal House* there's a picture of "U.S. Senator Blutarsky."

And that reminds me of Margaret Mead coming to campus. I went to see her with Jim. She wore a skirt and sat in an armchair onstage. She had big, wide, really enormous knees that looked like Bluto when he was getting ready to impersonate a zit.

There was a vogue for leading thinkers coming to campus. And for thinking that their thoughts led somewhere. And for Baby Boomers being smitten with them. Margaret Mead's knees were a distraction, but her presence was nonetheless intensely important. Self-consciousness is Baby Boom's salient trait, the crush is our signal emotion, and intense is our default mode.

Marshall McLuhan came to campus. The 1960s was an era of large thoughts. And yet, amazingly, each of those thoughts could fit on a T-shirt. The medium is the message. Buckminster Fuller came to campus too. (His nickname among architects was "Fuckminster Bullshit.") A couple of years later Timothy Leary was there. I was deeply impressed by his line of reasoning that was so convoluted even he couldn't follow it. Yes, I was stoned. But I walked away in awe that someone that old—he was in his forties—could still talk crazy talk. It gave me hope for the future. My hope for the future has not been disappointed, in this one respect.

Jim Fisk and I began hanging around at one of those old, large, and run-down houses rented to a constantly shuffled pack of students by landlords who have made a deal with the devil, the fire insurance company, and the county health department. Such houses in college towns were given names, perhaps because so much of college education has to do with naming things: ontogeny, phylogeny, Tappa Kegga Brew. This house was called Big Green after the color it had once been painted. Here in the prescribed disorder was the accustomed misbehavior and the requisite mayhem with the obligatory colorful characters.

Mostly it involved beer. But drugs were beginning to make an appearance or, rather, a smell. Now and then some of the tenants of the house would disappear mysteriously into the basement. A strong odor came up the stairs. The first time I visited I ran to the cellar door and yelled, "I think something's on fire down there!"

High, squeaky, hold-your-breath voices from below: "Everything's fine."

Jumbo was the first communist I'd ever met. From each according to his ability, to each according to his need. Jumbo needed beer.

Uncle Mike was a Physics grad student who spent a lot of time in the basement and a lot of the rest of the time in his room using Plexiglas, string, and felt-tipped markers to make models of four-dimensional cubes. Uncle Mike also liked handguns. And no matter what had gone on on Saturday night, he got up on Sunday morning, put on a suit, and went to Mass.

Dirty Eddie was the first hippie I'd ever met and the first person I'd ever heard say, "Oh, wow."

"It might rain."

"Oh, wow."

Dirty Eddie was letting all his fingernails grow, to see if he could.

Jack Hubert had been drafted and sent to Vietnam. He told us about the horrors of war. "The Vietnamese clap is the worst clap in the world. There are claw marks on the walls over all the urinals in Saigon from guys who got the Vietnamese clap."

Jack used his GI student benefits to buy a Norton Commando 750, which was supposed to be the fastest motorcycle made. The Norton was so aggressive-looking that it seemed like it could hurt you standing still. And with beer and faulty kickstand placement, it did just that to Jack.

There were parties at Big Green on Friday night and Saturday night and on Sunday night and Tuesday night and Thursday night, because smart people signed up for classes that met only on Tuesdays and Thursdays, and on Monday night and Wednesday night, because smart people signed up for classes that met after noon.

Sometimes the local bar band would bring its guitars and amplifiers, set up in the middle of the dining room, and perform "Tom Dooley" by the Kingston Trio, "Don't Let the Sun Catch You Crying" by Gerry and the Pacemakers, and "Paperback Writer" by the Beatles because these can be played with two chords.

Sometimes someone would suggest a "Mazola party" where everybody got naked in a heap on the floor and poured cooking oil all over themselves. But that much Mazola would cost a lot, and the floor was covered with cigarette butts and pop tops.

The next day everyone who was living in the house, or who was still there after the party, swept the floor. Under the front rooms of Big Green was a crawl space—twenty-five feet by twelve feet and four feet deep. A trap door opened into it. All the beer cans went down there. By June it was full. I calculate that during the 1965–66 school year we had 1,200 cubic feet of fun.

Our generation is identified with drugs, and even now the Baby Boom accords great significance (serotonin reuptake inhibitors) to drugs. But we never gave up on beer. We know what's good for us. Even when we were in our most hallucinogenic phase, we drank beer. Expanding your mind is like putting an addition on your house. You have to dig the stupid foundation first. And yet none of us has ever claimed that we've acquired happiness or peace of mind or wisdom or self-knowledge through beer. Nobody reads Aldous Huxley's *The Six-Pack of Perception*.

Are we being deliberately dishonest with ourselves? There's that Baby Boom thesis that postulates we can do anything. And on the subject of this thesis beer teaches important lessons. The next day.

Late one night we ran out of beer. Jack Hubert said he knew a place in the townie part of town where they sold moonshine. He returned with four mason jars. We drank them. I vomited. And I woke up blind. All I could see was blank white nothingness. I squinted. I blinked. Everything was white. There was a cold ring of pain around the top of my skull. "I drank moonshine and I'm blind!" I had passed out with my head upside down in the toilet.

What is love? 'tis not hereafter;
Present mirth hath present laughter;
What's to come is still unsure:
In delay there lies no plenty;
Then come kiss me, sweet and twenty,
Youth's a stuff will not endure.

—William Shakespeare,
Twelfth Night

12

ERA OF GOOD FEELINGS

If the sixties were the wild times we insist they were, we should have better stories. I blame it on drugs. When you drink beer a lot of things happen in the world. When you take drugs a lot of things happen in your head. Although sometimes the world and your head get mixed together. Once when I'd taken LSD I became convinced that Big Green's stairwell was the inside of an evil giant eel. If I went upstairs I'd be chewed by giant eel teeth. If I went downstairs I'd be eel shit. You spend a lot of your wild times just sitting there when you take drugs.

Dirty Eddie took drugs all the time. Not that he was inert. Sometimes he was busily to and fro in the world in a stoned way. He found a discarded floor-model console radio and somehow wrestled it back to Big Green and upstairs to his room. Plugged in, the radio received no broadcasts, but it's large, round dial lit up and its vacuum tubes produced a low hum.

The hum was, said Eddie, "*Om,* the cosmic sound of God." Eddie was a Hindu at the moment. He painted his room in saffron and red horizontal stripes. "Saffron," he said to anyone who would listen, "is the Vedic symbol of asceticism, and red is the Vedic symbol of sensuality." These wouldn't seem to go together, and they didn't because the two cans of paint that Eddie found on the discount table at the hardware store were icky yellow and dark pink.

Eddie painted the stripes freehand, beginning with the floorboards and going around the room over the woodwork, doors, light fixtures, window frames, window glass, curtains, and shades as high as he could reach, which left an additional stripe of flowered wallpaper visible beneath the crown moldings. The ultraviolet black light effects, the Day-Glo posters, and the lava lamps that people claim to remember from the 1960s would have been, comparatively, in restrained good taste.

Eddie also found, or purloined, a dozen metal folding chairs and arranged these facing the radio in what he called the "Om Theater." He sat in the front row, cross-legged on one of the chairs, hands templed at his sternum, humming along with the Philco. Nobody joined him. Dirty Eddie took to spending so much time in the Om Theater that the rest of us at Big Green forgot he was there.

Uncle Mike's room was next to Dirty Eddie's. Uncle Mike—so called for his avuncular way when urging others to use intoxicants and firearms—took drugs too. But he drank beer more often, especially when something was wrong with the world such as the Kaluza-Klein theory of five-dimensional cubes, President Johnson's proposed Gun Control Act, Vatican II, or a girl.

One day something was very wrong with the world. Uncle Mike returned from a long evening at the Final Exam, locked himself in his room, and expressed his *Weltschmerz* (or *Welt-Schlitz*, as it were) by firing a pistol into a wall about fifty times.

My girlfriend and I were downstairs and didn't pay much attention. It was a small-caliber pistol, and Uncle Mike had expressed himself before. We heard Uncle Mike unlock his door and walk, rather heavily, down the hallway toward the bathroom. Then there was a pause followed by screaming.

We ran upstairs. Dirty Eddie was lying on the pink and yellow floor in a tangle of chair legs.

"I killed him! I killed him! I killed him!" screamed Uncle Mike.

"I'm dead! I'm dead! I'm dead!" screamed Dirty Eddie.

"I shot through the wall and the bullets hit him!" screamed Uncle Mike.

"He shot through the wall and the bullets hit me!" screamed Dirty Eddie.

My girlfriend turned on the ceiling light. Eddie hadn't been able to get to it with his paintbrush. There didn't seem to be any blood on Dirty Eddie, although, what with the paint splatters all over his clothes, it was hard to tell.

I looked at the wall in Eddie's room. There were no bullet holes. I looked at the wall in Mike's room. There were plenty of bullet holes.

A weeping Uncle Mike was kneeling over a prostrate Dirty Eddie.

"I killed him!"

"I'm dead!"

"I killed him!"

"I'm dead!"

"Uncle Mike," I said, "the wall in Eddie's room doesn't have any bullet holes in it."

"Of course it doesn't," my girlfriend said. "Uncle Mike's closet is in between."

When Uncle Mike went to Mass on Sunday he could wiggle his fingers through the punctures in his suit coat pockets.

Of course this girlfriend at Big Green, Diane, was not the same girlfriend as the girlfriend in high school, Karen. We understand ourselves as an existential generation, creatures of here and now. Karen had an existential problem. She wasn't here now. Not that I didn't still love Karen, in the sixties sense of love, meaning fuck.

Once the Baby Boom had decided war was wrong and prejudice, poverty, and injustice should be eliminated and had gone to college, we began to understand ourselves as a noble generation. We had a right—*droit du seigneur*—to have sex and—*noblesse oblige*—an obligation to. Rights must be exercised in order to be preserved. We got a lot of exercise.

Diane was everything I desired. She laughed at my stories about how Al Bartz had commandeered the West Side High PA system. When Leo Luhan came for a visit from Big State she didn't make fun of him for falling down the trap door into the crawl space because he was wearing sunglasses indoors. She had—evidence indicated—fantasized about having sex with someone less tall and handsome than the boys on The Old School Cheer patio. In every imaginable position. She knew a dozen. If the sculptures she produced in Art class were anything to go by, she may have harbored a secret fondness for customizing plastic model cars.

Diane is my rod and my staff. We've been through the shadowed valleys, green pastures, and still waters. And the grandchildren are adorable. On another planet. In some different dimension. Out along one of those infinite tangents of choice that spun away in every direction from the perfect circle of the Baby Boom self.

I blame it on drugs. I don't blame drugs for what I did to Diane. I blame drugs for the other planet, the different dimension, and all the tangents the Baby Boom went off on. (And our spacey inclinations may explain why the Baby Boom wasn't as impressed with the 1969 moon landing as we should have been. "*Moon?*" we thought. "Everyone's gone to the moon.")

We weren't the first generation to fly around the room under the influence of pixie dust, act like fools with girls who called themselves "Tinker Bell" and "Tiger Lily," battle an imagined villain such as Hook—be he captain of pirate ship, industry, police force, or army—and string Wendy along for years while she yearned for a home and children of her own. But we were the generation that did it best.

Either we blame it on drugs or we blame it on ourselves. And let's not be silly.

For the middle-class, middle-America, middlingly hip Baby Boom, drugs arrived at the end of 1966. On Christmas break Jim Fisk, Tim Minsky, Ana Klein, Leo Luhan, and Al Bartz were in the finished basement at my house. We had a wooden matchbox completely full of pot. Joe Brody, as resident mischief maker, rightly should have been the one who "scored." Or Tim Minsky, home from with-it Yale. But it was premed Al Bartz.

"Organic Chem grad student," he said knowingly. Joe, however, figured out how to use the rolling papers.

Ana said, "All of existence is a dance."

". . . a pardon, a parole," said Joe.

". . . a lesson in organic chemistry," said Al.

". . . a proof of Fermat's theorem," said Tim. (And a Baby Boom mathematician would prove it, though not Tim Minsky.)

". . . a vindication of the rights of man," said Jim.

"Oh, wow," said Leo.

I said, "John Milton smoked pot," and got out my *Norton Anthology of English Literature* to prove it.

> *And Joy shall overtake us as a flood;*
> *When everything that is sincerely good*
> *And perfectly divine,*
> *With Truth, and Peace, and Love, shall ever shine . . .*
> *Then, all this earthy grossness quit,*
> *Attired with stars we shall for ever sit,*
> *Triumphing over Death, and Chance, and thee, O Time!*

We'd lost track of time. My mother came back from her bridge game, ran to the cellar door, and yelled, "I think something's on fire down there!"

Did drugs give the Baby Boom its taste for big ideas? More than enough big ideas were going around already in the sixties. Of the many big ideas I had on drugs, I can remember one. I had a sudden insight that there was a whole world outside me and a whole world inside me, and the outer world was no larger or more important than the inner world, but the inner world hadn't been explored, and society was telling me I could sail off the edge of it. So I took the *Nina,* the *Pinta,* the *Santa Maria* and some more LSD.

"I contain multitudes." Walt Whitman probably *did* take drugs, judging by the way his poetry scans. The word *epiphany* and the word *fantasy* have the same root in the Greek *phainein*, "to show." Psychedelic drugs put on quite a show.

Over the years I've asked old friends what effect drug taking had on the Baby Boom. When he got his first job selling boats, Billy Stumf said, "It's a great sales tool. I mean, for understanding the way customers think. I mean, you really don't know how stupid people are if you haven't taken drugs."

Back when we were still taking a lot of drugs, besides Lipitor, Jumbo said, "Drugs are the opiate of the masses." And added, "I'm a mass movement kind of guy."

Uncle Mike, who's been on the wagon since 1982, said, "It was just part of the fun. We were issued a lifetime supply of fun in the sixties. Although I went through mine pretty quick."

Tim Minsky said, "Drugs taught a generation of Americans the metric system." And who indeed knew what a kilo or a gram was before pot and coke began arriving in those quantities?

Jim Fisk said, "Drugs helped me with parenting by showing me how to lie to my children. I used to tell little lies. 'Oh, that old picture of Daddy with his hair all over the place? I was in a band. We played at folk Masses.' Then the kids got old enough to start asking about drugs. I realized I had to go big or go bust. 'I never took drugs. We thought drugs were really bad when I was at college. Drugs make people do embarrassing things and then the rush committee won't let you pledge Tappa Kegga Brew even though you're a legacy through Grandpa.'"

Jim is a writer. "Jim," I said, "you're a writer. You've written about taking drugs."

"Fortunately," he said, "the only people you can count on to never read anything you've written are your children." I'm counting on it myself.

Joe Brody said, "Drugs are a one-man birthday party. You don't get any presents you don't bring."

Al Bartz said drugs were a lesson in organic chemistry. "The brain is an organic chemistry factory. Baby Boomers with psychiatric problems know something's wrong with their brain chemistry. When I prescribe drugs for depression, anxiety, obsessive-compulsive disorder, or whatever, all my patients born before 1946 ask when they can get off drugs. All my patients born after 1946 ask when they can get more."

Leo Luhan said, "Oh, wow."

And Ana Klein said she couldn't make up her mind about the effect of drug taking on the Baby Boom. She wasn't sure whether it was a good thing or a bad thing, although drugs had put several boyfriends and two husbands out of the picture, and she wasn't sure whether that was a good thing or a bad thing either.

The sexual revolution was a bad thing. Imagine if what happened with sex and women in *the* sixties happened with golf and men in *their* sixties.

The Club is a wonderful place, with great facilities and a fabulous course. You'd always had a standing invitation to play there. But Club membership was restricted. No matter how often you'd been to Club events, and no matter how willingly you'd helped out with buffet suppers, table decorations, and cleaning up after the party, you couldn't join on your own.

Suddenly, you're a member. But it turns out you're expected to mow the fairways and tend the greens yourself and do all the Club's cooking and cleaning too. You not only get to play, you *have* to play. You're required to be in every foursome. (Well, let's not exaggerate—every twosome.) And abortion isn't legal yet, so no mulligans. (No cheap jokes about Hole-in-One tournaments either.)

We never thought of our 1960s sexual excursions as causing us to lose our bearings in our 1960s political movements or make detours in our 1960s spiritual journeys. We must have had quite a map. (And not for nothing was the word *trip* overused in the sixties.)

Beginning our mystical jaunt, we carried very little luggage. The only religious idea that any of us seemed to remember from going through the motions and maintaining the forms at Sunday school was a phrase of the Apostle John's from a part of the New Testament that even Johnny MacKay hadn't had to read. The First Epistle General of John, chapter 4, verse 8: "God is love." Oddly, the Jewish kids seemed to remember it too, which says something about the well-intentioned homogeneity of 1950s American culture, although I don't know what it says, because not long after we learned God is love we learned love in the sixties sense.

These things I command you, that ye fuck one another. Thou shalt fuck thy neighbor as thyself. Better is a dinner of herbs where a fuck is, than a stalled ox back home with your parents. Greater love hath no woman than this, that a woman lay down with everybody. So faith, hope, and love abide, but the greatest of these is a blow job. For God so fucked the world . . .

We are a unitary generation, determined that the physical, the metaphysical, and the intellectual be brought together, not to say get all mixed up. We recognize no separation of minds, spirits, and bodies. Especially bodies. Or we didn't until Baby Boom feminists read the riot act to Baby Boom chauvinists during the divorce. After that only one body occupied the physical house and the bank account became metaphysical because the intellectual lawyer had to be paid.

But forty-some years ago the Baby Boom could be observed in its unadulterated (a pun on adultery is lurking in there) state—trying to get to all the places no one had ever been before and hoping to get enlightened, stoned, and laid in all those places at the same time. "Dear Mom and Dad, I'm trying to find myself. I think I might be in San Francisco. Please send airfare."

Of course this is a sweeping generalization about the Baby Boom. More than enough sweeping generalizations are going around already in this book. A unitary generation we may have been. A unified generation we weren't. Many Baby Boomers were almost normal. Sometimes, in moments of doubt, one wonders if there's really such a thing as a Baby Boom generation at all. For example, everything I have to say about the sixties Baby Boom is what, in deductive logic, is called "fallacy of the undistributed middle term." To put it into a syllogism:

> Major proposition: In 1967 everyone between the age of 21 and the age of 3 was a member of the Baby Boom.
>
> Minor proposition: I was nuts.
> _____
> Conclusion: What a generation!

Or, using inductive logic, I'm thinking about the six of us who grew up at the same end of the block: Billy and Bobby Stumf, Johnny MacKay, Steve Penske, Jerry Harris, and me. We were a pretty good statistical sample, being randomly acquainted in a random city in that random state Ohio. We were a socioeconomic cross section. We weren't really. But in those days everybody who wasn't considered normal was considered abnormal. Being black and poor and other things meant you were a "statistical outlier." And, in fact, we were an economic cross section of a kind. Suburbia had not begun its meritocratic sorting of educated elites from people who lift things. David Brooks wasn't born yet.

Susie Inwood's dad was a postman. Mr. Biedermeyer was assistant superintendant of schools. Mr. Stumf sold (strangely or aptly, considering how he'd risked his life in World War II and Korea) life insurance. My dad sold cars. Mr. MacKay owned a printing company. Mr. Penske was a telephone lineman. Mr. Harris managed the produce department at a grocery store.

The six of us were all boys, which leaves out half of the Baby Boom. But that was the sixties for you. See sexual revolution above.

Steve Penske died young. He accidentally drowned while fishing. Dying young was a very sixties thing to do. But while fishing? Johnny MacKay stayed born-again and not because of cancer, jail, or a 12-step program (or those wet baptismal gowns) but because he believed what he'd been taught, which is never a sufficient excuse with our generation. Jerry Harris didn't go to West Side High. He went to Central Tech. He never attended college. And he learned a trade. Thus there is no part for him to play in the sixties Baby Boom narrative—François Villon escaping the gallows to be an apprentice plumber. Bobby Stumf volunteered for Vietnam, returned to our hometown, and became a policeman. That leaves me and Billy Stumf, who was selling boats the last I heard. And I've lost touch with Billy.

But who wants logic? Being logical would have wrecked the sixties. The sixties were so creative. Being logical wrecks every form of creativity. Hamlet lets it slide. Lady Macbeth says, "Oh, listen to you, big Thane of Cawdor. Enough already with the social climbing." Iago talks trash about Desdemona, TLC makes a reality TV show about it, everybody gets paid a fortune, and Othello becomes a spokesperson for a national campaign against family violence.

Anyway, sweeping generalizations about 1960s sexual excursions, political movements, and spiritual journeys are all right. It's not as if we got very far on most of our trips.

We were thrown out of Big Green because the owner was, quite rightly, tearing the place down. Also, we hadn't paid the rent. Jumbo found us a farmhouse for $125 a month. "The guerrilla must move among the peasants as a fish swims in the sea," Jumbo said, quoting Chairman Mao.

Not that Jumbo went outdoors much. And the peasants were Republican.

Uncle Mike got ahold of some dynamite. In those days you could buy dynamite and fuses and blasting caps at the feed and grain store, for blowing up stumps. We didn't have a stump, but Uncle Mike thought that just the blowing up part would be a trip.

We were stoned. We'd been sitting on the front porch all afternoon smoking hashish until the world had slowed to a crawl. Uncle Mike seemed to take forever inserting the blasting cap into the stick of dynamite and the fuse into the blasting cap. Finally he had the cap crimped and his Zippo ready, and he began to walk out into the hayfield the farmhouse had instead of a yard. He walked and he walked. And he walked and walked and walked. At last, far, far away, he put the dynamite down in the grass. There was a slow stoop and a long pause and a brilliant little spark visible in the extreme distance as he lit the fuse. Then Mike began to run back to the house. He ran and ran. He kept running. He seemed to be taking forever to run. And just as he put his foot on the porch step the dynamite exploded.

There was an immense shower of plants and dirt. Uncle Mike was driven into Jumbo and both went through the screen in the screen door. Diane was sitting on the porch swing and was propelled back over the railing and almost dumped in the forsythia. The hash pipe was pushed out of Dirty Eddie's teeth and into his face leaving a blister on the end of his nose. Several windows were broken. Some shingles were blown off the porch roof. Uncle Mike had planted the dynamite five feet from the house.

To flaming youth let virtue be as wax.

—William Shakespeare,
Hamlet

13

THE BABY BOOM'S GARDEN OF EDEN——THANKS FOR THE SNAKE

Were the sixties primarily a political phenomenon? Were the sixties primarily a cultural phenomenon? Were the sixties primarily a social phenomenon? Don't ask us.

In the sixties the Baby Boom was the tailgate party, not the team on the field. There was a lot of "talkin' 'bout my generation" (Pete Townshend, born 1945), but it wasn't *my* generation that was causing "What's Going On" (Marvin Gaye, born 1939) during the "Youthquake" (a coinage from *Punch*, edited by people born when mastodons roamed the earth). A birth year checklist tells the story.

Bob Dylan, 1941
John Lennon, 1940

Mick Jagger, 1943
Timothy Leary, 1920
Ken Kesey, 1935
R. Crumb, 1943
Peter Max, 1937
Bernardine Dohrn, 1942
Bill Ayers, 1944
Che Guevara, 1928
Malcolm X, 1925
Muhammad Ali, 1942
Abbie Hoffman, 1936
Jane Fonda, 1937
Gloria Steinem, 1934
Jimi Hendrix, 1942
Jerry Garcia, 1942
Chairman Mao, 1893

I guess to fully understand what it was like to be young in the 1960s you had to not be. The Silent Generation, as usual, was producing the loudest noise. The most influential sixties scene makers who were actually members of the Baby Boom were Donovan (1946) and Twiggy (1949).

We aren't the generation of the Beatles and the Rolling Stones, expanded consciousness, the New Left, Black Power, or Women's Liberation. We're the generation of the fanboy (Jann Wenner, 1946), Grand Funk Railroad (all born in the early 1950s), and Ben & Jerry (both born in 1951).

As their ice cream attests (go for the Butter Pecan, skip the Phish Food), the Baby Boom enjoys its luxuries. And what is more luxurious than knowing something wasn't our fault? Especially something like the sixties.

*   *   *

It was a comic interlude—in a century that needed one. Not that we didn't take being ridiculous seriously. That was part of the fun. You can goof off at work, but you can't goof off at goofing off. Fun engages your attention.

"The personal is the political" was a fun idea. Not that we goof-offs used the phrase at the time, any more than we called ourselves "hippies" (Dirty Eddie excepted) or claimed that "What's Going On" was a "Youthquake." The personal/political slogan came a little later, from the feminists, once they'd realized they should be pissed off about the sexual revolution (and everything else). But we got the idea. Politics was all about me.

We the Me of the United States, in Order to form a more perfect Me, establish Just Me, insure domestic Tranquility (Diane had moved in with Me), provide for defense of Me (Uncle Mike had guns), promote going on Welfare (if it came to that for Me), and secure the Blessing of Liberty to Me and Abortion Rights for my Posterity, do ordain and establish this Constitution for Me!

Jim Fisk's Constitutional Law class had happily degenerated into an hour-long, three-times-a-week shouting match about the war in Vietnam. It is difficult, at this late date, to explain who was shouting at whom and about what.

The professor opposed the war in Vietnam and the students opposed the war in Vietnam except for one holdout coed whose fiancé was a marine lieutenant in Vietnam, and she was too cute to shout at. But, in politics as in life, once things get personal a lot of shouting ensues.

The professor, who'd once had something to do with Adlai Stevenson's presidential campaign, possibly involving yard signs, believed in fighting communism by diplomatic engagement, addressing the individual aspirations of indigenous Marxist political movements, playing upon the contradictions and rivalries within the Sino-Soviet bloc. "You don't understand," he would shout. "Yugoslavia is the future!"

The students believed the Vietcong hated LBJ almost as much as we did. Jack Hubert said the pot in Vietnam was amazing. And the Vietcong had that cool name, like with a fistful of Lyndon Johnson instead of Fay Wray and Huey helicopters instead of biplanes, hanging in there on top of a monument to greedy materialism. They were obviously the good guys, or would be the good guys, if they'd stop trying to kill the cute coed's fiancé and he'd stop trying to kill them, war being wrong.

"War is wrong!" a pacifist student would shout at an activist student.

"Imperialism is wrong!" the activist student would shout back.

"Neocolonialism is wrong!" a leftist student would shout at both of them. "Amerika [the lefist students such as Jumbo were able to get the *k* in there verbally] is waging war on Vietnam [pronounced "*Viet*nahm" if you were against the war and "Viet *Nam*" if you were for it] to exploit Vietnamese natural resources!"

Which, nowadays, would have brought the shouting to a halt while somebody Googled to see if Vietnam has any. But Larry Page and Sergey Brin hadn't invented Google yet. They're a couple of those Generation X slackers who had to come up with Google because they lacked the Baby Boom gumption for a real shouting match, if you ask me. And you'll note that Google never settles a Baby Boom shouting match anyway; it just causes a brief, smug pause.

"Natural resources like rice!" someone else would shout. "The company that owns Uncle Ben's rice is part of the military-industrial complex like Dow Chemical that produces Saran Wrap and napalm!"

"Uncle Ben is a racist stereotype!"

"War is wrong because Saran Wrap exploits black people!"

"My fiancé is in Viet *Nam*!"

Jim said, "I had to raise my voice to a shout in Constitutional Law class to point out that the war is unconstitutional —Article I, section 8."

When the bell rang everyone left to smoke pot, often at the professor's house. Except for the cute coed. She went back to her sorority. Although they were starting to smoke pot there too.

Dirty Eddie founded a commune on the farm we were renting, at the other end of the hayfield from the dynamite hole. The generation that had bitterly protested even the slightest of yard work chores decided, for a moment, to go back to the land. There was only one vegetable the commune had any success growing, until they got paranoid after seeing a sheriff's department car go by the end of the farm's driveway and smoked the single plant when it was three inches tall.

The commune members were building wigwams, teepees, yurts, and geodesic domes. Although it was difficult to tell which was supposed to be what. These structures were held together with tangled skeins of cordage and big snarls of rope tied in hopeless clumps of failed half hitches, sheet bends, and bowlines. As I mentioned earlier, the Boy Scouts had not engaged the Baby Boom's attention.

Whenever it rained or the wind blew or they needed to go to the bathroom or get a drink of water or cook something, the commune members were, quite communistically, in our house. Jumbo said they should study Kim Il Sung's North Korean doctrine of *Juche,* or self-reliance, and go rely on themselves in their yurts. The fact that North Korea is still around indicates that Kim Il Sung was not a fellow member of Bat Patrol, Troop 44, with me and Steve Penske, in the Methodist church gymnasium. Dirty Eddie's commune lasted a month.

It was a decade without quality control. And it was not, of course, a decade. The "sixties" as they are popularly remembered—what might too well be called "The High Sixties"—was an episode of about seventy-two months' duration that started in 1967 when the Baby Boom had fully infested academia and America's various little bohemian enclaves such as Greenwich Village, Haight-Ashbury, Big Sur, and the finished basement at my house and came to an abrupt halt in 1973 when conscription ended and herpes began.

Meanwhile all dreck broke loose. There was the music. We must not be deceived into nostalgia. The word is from the Greek *nostos,* to come home, and *algos,* pain. Let us recall what a pain we were when we came home and turned up "In-A-Gadda-Da-Vida" by Iron Butterfly on the stereo in the finished basement.

Do what you can to banish from your mind all balmy impressions of the sixties. Fill out a tax form. Have a phone chat with your insurance agent. Play *Grand Theft Auto V* with an eight-year-old nephew. Get a prostate exam. Now listen to a Jerry Garcia guitar solo.

As Al Bartz put it in 1973, "What did the Grateful Dead fan say when he ran out of pot?"

"What a shitty band."

Andy Warhol was a revelation, though not his Marilyn Monroe portraits. (The Baby Boom never understood Marilyn Monroe as a sex object—too much of an adult fantasy for a perpetually young generation. Although a few of us understood her as a role model if we wanted to dress up as somebody our mother was jealous of and die tragically.) It was the Brillo and the Campbell's soup that we liked. Artistic brilliance was right there staring us in the face. Everything was artistic. And anybody could be artistically brilliant.

Diane's art class started turning out paintings of Kleenex boxes, Dixie cups, Lifebuoy soap bars, Prell shampoo tubes, and Ban aerosol deodorant cans. The lettering is surprisingly hard to do in egg tempera.

There was a poet in those days, Aram Saroyan, son of the novelist and playwright William Saroyan. Here is an Aram Saroyan poem:

priit

That's all. That's the whole thing. Aram Saroyan received a grant from the National Endowment for the Arts.

I was nominated for a grant myself, a fellowship to go to graduate school. A professor put me up for it, and not the one smoking pot with Jim Fisk's Constitutional Law class. My ambition was to write incomprehensible novels, although James Joyce seemed to have a lock on that, so maybe I'd write incomprehensible poetry. I was sure I could do it in greater quantity than Aram Saroyan. Then, as now, graduate school was thought to be the route to such glory.

I submitted the requisite essay in incomprehensible prose and received a letter saying I was a finalist for the fellowship. The winner would be decided by a committee of five academic worthies, who would interview each finalist at Big State University.

I arrived at Big State the night before my interview and went out beer drinking and pot smoking with Leo Luhan and Joe Brody until dawn. I was supposed to be at Big State's English Department at 9 a.m. I came to on the couch in Leo's apartment at 9:15, pulled on my Schlitz-drenched blue jeans and work shirt reeking of sinsemilla, and rushed unwashed, uncombed, and unshaven to the campus. I was shown into a seminar room and placed on a hard chair facing a table behind which sat the five academic worthies, each with a notepad. I remember only one of the questions.

WORTHY: Which literary critic has had the most profound influence on your thinking?

ME: . . .

I could not think of the name of a single literary critic. Not John Crowe Ransom, not Cleanth Brooks, not R. P. Blackmur, not even Leon Edel from whom I'd cribbed my junior thesis on Henry James. (Joyce was too incomprehensible.)

ME: Henry David Thoreau.

WORTHIES (*more or less in unison*): Henry David Thoreau wasn't a literary critic.

ME: His whole *life* was an act of literary criticism.

I got the fellowship.

*   *   *

It took all the Baby Boom qualities to make a successful sixties. Maybe we were only the tailgate party but let us not forget that the tailgate party is where the fun is and that tailgate-party personal interaction is of broader and deeper social significance than what the quarterback is up to.

At the 1968 Democratic Convention in Chicago, Baby Boom political protesters stopped in the middle of getting whacked with police billy clubs to chant "The Whole World Is Watching!" What other political protesters would have paused to announce the importance of their self-image instead of fighting back or running like hell?

What other hopeless romantics could feel, the way the Baby Boom did, such unrequited love for inanimate objects—and not sailing ships, fast trains, or speeding automobiles but inanimate objects that were good for nothing but conking us on the head like Dirty Eddie's geodesic dome and lysergic acid diethylamide?

What other pious acolytes were ever so earnestly convinced in their faith as we who believed that there is a transmigration of souls (if they're going to San Francisco), that all things are one (or two, if she's a babe), that Jim Morrison is a poet, Hubert Humphrey is a Nazi, Diane's best friend is a witch, and Transcendental Meditation isn't just sitting there?

Our salient trait is self-consciousness, our signal emotion is the crush, our default mode is intense, but our genius is being funny. We just didn't know it yet.

Not even, especially not, at Woodstock. The long weekend of August 15–17, 1969, was the Baby Boom's great where-weren't-you? moment. Along with 75,550,000 other Baby Boomers, where I wasn't was at Woodstock.

Though not for lack of trying. The eternal love of my life, that month, was Chloe Dobsonberg, a raven-haired, more exotic version of Marsha Matthiessen. Chloe attended Pricey College for Women, a very liberal arts school next door to Mediocre State.

Chloe had a Pre-Raphaelite upper lip, fully, lusciously coiled back on itself in carnal invitation. I have never seen a Pre-Raphaelite upper lip on another living woman, Botox do what it will. I knew this was a Pre-Raphaelite lip, I had taken Art History (or "Darkness at Noon," as it was called) because the class met only on Tuesdays and Thursdays. One of the slides in the Art History slide show was Dante Gabriel Rossetti's *Persephone* who looked just like Chloe Dobsonberg except, fortunately, Chloe didn't have Persephone's great big nose. Hers was cutely pug.

Chloe lived in exotic Massapequa, Long Island. I came east by motorcycle with the idea of Chloe riding pillion to a "Woodstock Music and Arts Fair," which, according to a poster in a record shop in Yellow Springs, Ohio, was to be "An Aquarian Exposition" featuring "Three Days of Peace and Music." I pictured something on the order of a wind chime sale with evening hootenannies and maybe a surprise guest appearance by Mimi Fariña.

Chloe, alas, chose the Sunday prior to make a feeble gesture at doing away with herself. (Such feeble gestures were more or less obligatory among students at liberal arts women's colleges in the sixties—too much reading of Sylvia Plath poems is my guess. There was an old stone bridge on the PCW campus from which at least one student per semester would plunge. The drop was less than three yards into a foot-deep duck pond.)

While her parents were out slicing Titleists and lobbing Wilsons, Chloe emptied the family medicine cabinet, swallowing upward of a half a dozen Midol, One A Day, and Miltown tablets. There was a crash of Cadillacs backing into each other as mom, dad, aunts, et cetera, raced from the parking lot of the Massapequa golf club, Par Venu Links. Ambulances were called. A tummy was pumped. (A rather cute little tummy, if memory serves.)

I was deeply upset because Chloe's suicide attempt was the result of a fight with her mother about a Bloomingdale's charge plate bill for a $108 fringed suede vest with genuine Native American beadwork and had nothing to do with Chloe's desperate romantic feelings for me.

I was also slightly disappointed about missing Woodstock until the nightly news reported that it had turned into a catastrophic, drug-addled, rain-drenched disaster area lacking food, shelter, drinking water, and Porta Potties. Then I was furious about missing Woodstock.

What this says about Baby Boomers I needn't tell anyone who raised, was married to, or has ever known one.

A few years ago, on the fortieth anniversary of too many people needing haircuts going to an upstate New York dairy farm for no good reason, I paged through some of the books published to commemorate the occasion.

The books have photographs, particularly nude photographs. Two facts are evident. The gym had not been discovered. And the ratio of boys to girls at Woodstock was of almost

Castro District proportions. At least the fellows on Castro Street didn't go there hoping to meet girls. Woodstock looks sad and drab and inspirational only in an "Every Litter Bit Hurts" way.

But Woodstock had tremendous cultural impact. In one of the books, one of the event's promoters, Michael Lang, says, "The lighting of candles would set a precedent that carries on to this day. The candles became lighters, which have since become cell phones."

And Woodstock had tremendous political impact. "Out of that sense of community, out of that vision, that Utopian vision, comes the energy to go out there and actually participate in the process so that social change occurs," Abbie Hoffman is quoted as saying shortly before he killed himself. In the meantime Abbie had written a book, *Woodstock Nation*. Like everybody else, I've never read it, but later I'd go to this country—overcrowded, muddy, lacking in food and public order. It's called Bangladesh. (Wasn't there another concert having something to do with that place?)

And Woodstock had tremendous socioeconomic impact. In another book, another of the event's promoters, Artie Kornfeld, says, "That mud was like heavenly water washing away all that was wrong with the world at that time." In case you were wondering where the 1970s came from.

The be-in required some "Be All You Can Be." The Woodstock books praise the National Guard for using its helicopters to deliver donated food and medevac attendees. No mention is made of the mission the National Guard would accomplish the following spring at Kent State.

But there was all that wonderful music—the Doors (not there), Led Zeppelin (not there), the Byrds (not there), the Moody Blues (not there), Jethro Tull (not there), Joni Mitchell (not there but wrote "We've Got to Get Ourselves Back to the Garden" after she heard about it), and Melanie (there but didn't write "Lay Down (Candles in the Rain)" until someone told her she'd been there).

Less well remembered for playing at Woodstock were people who played at Woodstock—Bert Sommer, the Keef Hartley Band, Sweetwater, a group called Quill with a song called "That's How I Eat," and Country Joe McDonald without the Fish, a McDonald's Happy Meal without the toy.

The show opened with three hours of Richie Havens. That's a lot of "Handsome Johnny," but the other performers had not yet arrived. There was no one to follow Havens. Michael Lang got an idea: "My old friend Peter Max . . . had brought the swami." Swami Satchidananda was duly trotted onstage. "He put a wave of peace out there," said Artie Kornfeld.

Snigger, if you will, about Swami Satchidananda's wave of peace, but the crowd did not murder sitar virtuoso Ravi Shankar when he played "Raga Puriya-Danashri/Gat in Sawaritai," which, if it was as long as its title, must have tried the patience of even the most blissfully stoned.

And Jimi Hendrix's famous psychedelic rendition of the "Star-Spangled Banner" was performed at 8:30 on Monday morning when everyone who was able to leave Woodstock had done so.

Not many epoch-defining phenomena can be completely analyzed, thoroughly critiqued, and given their entire historical due in just one word. Except Woodstock. Altamont.

However, I've looked up the birth dates of the four people who organized (if that word can possibly be used here) Woodstock—Michael Lang, Artie Kornfeld, John Roberts, and Joel Rosenman. None of them was a Baby Boomer. So, once again, we have the luxury (a luxury that grows rarer and rarer now that we're over fifty) of knowing it wasn't our fault.

You must, therefore, confess that by "individual" you mean no other person than the bourgeois, than the middle-class owner of property. This person must, indeed, be swept out of the way and made impossible.

—Karl Marx and Friedrich Engels,
The Communist Manifesto

14

THERE SHALL NO SIGN BE GIVEN UNTO THIS GENERATION

The sixties produced various enigmas. One of which isn't: Why were Baby Boomers acting like chuckleheads? Because we could.

But the Vietnam War remains a puzzle. Not that there was anything puzzling about why we opposed it. The Baby Boom was having a party, and the Vietnam War interrupted it. Try it yourself. Go to a beer blast at midnight and suggest all the guys leave, get buzz cuts, and do push-ups.

Joe Brody, who wasn't quite clinging to a draft deferment grade average, said, "The government wants to send me to a distant place to shoot people I've never met. And they're expected to shoot back. How come the government doesn't want to send me to my house to shoot my drunk stepfather while he's snoring on the couch?"

Inner-city rioting was another puzzle. We were all for Black Power, but we were perplexed. Why were they burning their homes instead of ours? I never got up the nerve to ask any of the black students at MSU. There weren't many, and most of them were football players. Possibly they weren't very radical, but definitely they were very big.

Our antiwar demonstrations, where we showed more talent for running around and squealing than for violence, were puzzling too. We thought that if we dressed like zanies, acted like Vancouver Canuck fans after the Boston Bruins won the 2011 Stanley Cup, and came up with chants that rhymed better than "The Whole World Is Watching" such as "Hey, Hey, LBJ! How Many Kids Did You Kill Today?" we'd stop the war.

Mostly, we were just enjoying ourselves. The Vietnam War was a permission slip for nice middle-class kids to mock authority figures, vandalize property, and get chased by the police. Then we'd watch ourselves on TV and some authority figure with lots of property who had never been chased by the police in his life would come on and say we were "The Conscience of the Nation." Plus it was a great way to meet girls. I'd get all covered in tear gas with some girl who called herself Sunshine and go back to her place, and I'd say, "We'd better double up in the shower, Sunshine, to conserve earth's resources."

Given how long the Vietnam War dragged on, this didn't work. On the other hand, people aren't enjoying themselves very much protesting the war in Afghanistan, and that's dragged on even longer.

*　　*　　*

Jumbo—actually Arthur—said Karl Marx explained all this. Jumbo was called Jumbo because he was a large presence as well as a large person; also his last name was Jumbold. Maybe Jumbo really had read Karl Marx, although he was known to be a kidder. Ana Klein brought back reports from Selective State about students who read Karl Marx and argued, for many hours, about whether they were Marxist-Leninists or Trotskyites or Maoists and whether they should get a haircut to campaign for Gene McCarthy.

Jumbo, Dirty Eddie, Jim Fisk (who actually did get a haircut to campaign for Gene McCarthy), Uncle Mike, Diane, and I had arguments like that, for a few minutes, until Uncle Mike got out the rolling papers and the argument became about how many pizzas to order.

Jumbo said, while we were waiting for pizza, "Karl Marx explains everything."

Diane asked, "Why would anybody want everything explained?" It's a sensible question that should have been pondered then and still should be now. Diane was a sensible woman, even if her best friend was a witch (and wicked in bed, I'm ashamed to report).

Jumbo said (high, squeaky, hold-your-breath voice), "*I could have explained a few minutes ago.*"

Diane said (high, squeaky, hold-your-breath voice), "*You shouldn't believe everything you think.*"

Which is yet another mystery of the sixties. Why did we think we were such big ideological left-wingers? The political left, always on the lookout for more people with a beef, had been good on civil rights issues. The left's neocolonialist Saran

Wrap exploitation analysis of the Vietnam War did include that it stank. And, of course, we agreed with the left that everybody should have lots of everything except for people who have lots of everything who should have it taken away. That's just human nature.

But what really appealed to us in leftist politics was the politics, the quantity of the politics. As Jumbo was about to explain, before Uncle Mike got out the rolling papers, the left makes everything political. And anybody can get into politics—look at the people who do. The threshold is low. The skill set is easy. The power—"How Many Kids Did You Kill Today?"—is enormous. Put absolutely everything together with absolutely anybody in some absolutist system—Marxist-Leninism, Trotskyism, Maoism, Social Democratic Welfare State, whatever—and . . .

Jim Fisk said (high, squeaky, hold-your-breath voice), "*We can do anything!*"

Plus, among the various ways that self-with-a-hyphen can be used to describe the Baby Boom (112 by my count in *Webster's Third International*), there is self-righteous. We were looking under every rock for moral high ground to stand on. By being big ideological left-wingers we could oppose prejudice, poverty, war, and injustice *and* annoy our parents.

Although not my grandmother. I came home from college disorderly, disheveled, and hirsute, with a big red fist stenciled on the back of my jean jacket. Grandma was old enough to remember when men of dignity and consequence sported the wild and woolly in a way that would have done Friedrich Engels proud. She was farm girl enough to recall men being customarily dirty. But she was concerned about my prattle on public affairs.

"Pat," she said, "are you becoming a Democrat?"

"Grandma!" I said. "Lyndon Johnson and Richard Nixon are both fascist pigs! Of course I'm not a Democrat! I'm a communist!"

"Well, just as long as you're not a Democrat."

When Martin Luther King, Jr. was assassinated the black students at MSU held a memorial in the quad at the center of the campus. They wore black armbands. Black armbands were not readily available at college town haberdasheries. They tied black dress socks around their arms.

Jumbo was the only one who felt sufficient confidence in his proletarian solidarity to mention it. "A marketing ploy for Gold Toe over-the-calf length men's socks, at a moment like this. Truly capitalism is evil," he said, although not within the hearing of any black students.

As a comic interlude the sixties was not always a success. There were inner-city riots after the assassination. There were inner-city riots every summer. There were even inner-city riots where I came from, which wasn't a big enough city to fit an inner- into it. There was, however, the black neighborhood on the south side between downtown and the rail yards. (The school system, really thinking that one through, had christened the South Side High School sports teams the Rebels, and generations of black students had a high school newspaper named *The Rebel Yell*.)

On the other side of the rail yards, just outside the city limits, was Polack Town or, as it was called if you were talking to someone who was Polish ("sensitive speech" wasn't invented yesterday), Polish Village.

My high school girlfriend Karen was Polish. Karen, being on the same good terms with her parents as most college kids were at that time, was staying with her grandmother in Polack Town.

She could see the fires and hear the sirens on the other side of the railroad tracks. I thought I should be there and do something, although I can't imagine what. If the rioting spilled over from the south side maybe I could express proletarian solidarity.

A curfew was in force. But there was a back way to Polack Town through city park service roads and down some alleys. I took the family car and drove to Karen's grandmother's house. Polack Town's little front yards were filled with men holding their duck guns. Normally I would have been subject to catcalls or worse from these fellows for wearing my hair like Veronica Lake. But this evening I was white.

I was too confused by getting a glimpse of what revolution might be like to realize I was getting a glimpse of what revolution might be like.

You say you want a revolution is something that could have been said, if we'd known the Beatles personally, to Jumbo and me and Dirty Eddie and Uncle Mike and even Karen although she was more interested in heightening hem lines than heightening class contradictions.

The expression of the day that nicely triangulated excitement, fear, and being stupid was "flipped out." (Not to be confused with "freaked out," which triangulated excitement, paranoia, and being stoned.) Karen was flipped out about the south side riots. I was flipped out about the Polack Town front yards. Karen's grandmother had lived in the part of Poland that had had the Russians come in and the Germans come in and the Germans go out and the Russians come back in. She said, "Would you like some pierogi?"

*   *   *

Over in Indochina, where actual revolutionaries were involved, things weren't going well either. Maybe Vietnam was the Greatest Generation attempting to practice homeopathy on Cold War ills. A small dose of what makes you sick will cure you, so they had a little war instead of mutually assured destruction.

Or maybe the Greatest Generation was trying to be imaginative with the Cold War, like Jim Fisk's Constitutional Law professor, addressing the individual aspirations of indigenous Marxist political movements, with napalm. As mentioned, imagination was not the Greatest Generation's strong point. They should have stuck to cars. The 1958 Edsel was so terrifyingly imaginative that my dad, who was in the business and knew the sales manager of the local Edsel dealership, said they hadn't been able to sell a single one. The front end looked like one of those creatures that deep-sea explorers saw out the window of a bathysphere. Dropping a 1958 Edsel on Hanoi might have given Ho Chi Minh second thoughts.

Or maybe the Greatest Generation was modeling its war against communism in Southeast Asia on its war against Dutch elm disease in the Midwest. We had a puny maple at our house, but the older homes in the neighborhood were shaded by enormous elms. They were swell climbing trees with thick limbs branching off low from the trunk, within a boy's easy reach. Jerry Harris got his foot caught in the crotch of an elm and was stuck for hours because the only way he could get loose was by untying his shoe and leaving it there. Losing a shoe was an offense punishable by a Gulf of Tonkin Resolution on your behind. Anyway, when

Dutch elm disease struck, the city council responded by cutting down all the elms in the city, and the disease was completely eradicated.

Jumbo was imaginative in his organization of an antiwar protest at MSU. When the campus bell tower's bells rang at noon on May first, student antiwar protesters flushed all the school's toilets at the same time. There were strong objections from students who were not protesting and were in the gymnasium showers. Jumbo was expelled and got drafted.

He was philosophical about it. "If I don't go, one of the proletariat will have to go in my place and I'm one of the proletariat so I'm going in place of myself."

"Jumbo," said Diane, "the only job you've ever had was at Varsity Pizza Pie, and you were fired for eating too much of the pizza."

"In communist society, accumulated labor is but a means to widen, to enrich, to promote the existence of the laborer," said Jumbo, quoting *The Communist Manifesto*. "And," he added, "I'll be in the belly of the beast."

"I see the belly part," said Diane.

"I'll work from within to end the war," said Jumbo. "My strategy is fraternization with the masses."

This was the same strategy Jumbo had advocated for inner-city riots in Jim Fisk's Constitutional Law class.

"When the Eighty-second Airborne was sent into Detroit," Jumbo had said, "they should have brought some of that amazing pot from Vietnam with them. Everything would have been cool."

Everything didn't seem to be cool in Vietnam, amazing pot or no. In Detroit 43 people were killed and 412 buildings were burned. Maybe amazing pot would have made the gunfire less accurate and also limited the arson, if trying to keep a joint lit is anything to go by. Jumbo was getting an A in Constitutional Law before he was expelled.

"Judging by Jack Hubert's stories about the clap," Jumbo said, "fraternization with the masses has already progressed to a high degree."

"Wear a rubber," said Diane.

Jumbo did well in basic training. "Graduated with high Marx"—his joke, not mine, on a postcard from Fort Dix. When he was given a form allowing him to state a preference for specialized training he discovered that the Army Blimp Corps still existed and checked that box. The army assigned him to forward air control instead.

Jumbo sat in the back of a little tandem-seat propeller plane, a modified Cessna 170, never mind his bulk. The plane, barely faster than the Edsel that should have been dropped on Ho Chi Minh, flew low over the jungle looking for things to be bombed or shelled. Jumbo's plane was shot down and he was killed.

Glendower: I can call spirits from the vasty deep.
Hotspur: Why, so can I, or so can any man; But will they come when you do call for them?

—William Shakespeare,
Henry IV, Part 1

15

DAWN'S EARLY LIGHT

You can't make a joke out of everything. But you can keep trying. Those of us, at least those of us who dodged the draft and who were still adrift along the Baby Boom's infinite tangents of choice, were doing a pretty good job of it with our own lives.

I came east to graduate school in Baltimore at Ivy Wannabe University where I was enrolled in its not very renowned Writers Workshop. This met twice a week and most of the class period was devoted, disappointingly, to the other workshop students reading aloud from their incomprehensible prose and poetry instead of me reading aloud from mine. In my spare time, which is to say all but eight waking hours per month, I was writing long rants about bourgeois pigs for an underground newspaper called *Puddles*. ("Fascist pigs" was the way I put it, although the Greatest Generation had done so well at wiping out fascist pigs that there weren't enough left to go around.)

I probably was, personally, getting too far out on the Baby Boom's antiestablishmentarian freaky vector. I mean, not weird heavy twisted freaky far out like some poor benighted Baby Boomers such as Linda Kasabian, Susan Atkins, Patricia Krenwinkel, and Squeaky Fromme. (Talk about having an ultimately disappointing relationship with the Silent Generation—Charles Manson was born in 1934.)

Joe Brody, on the other hand, gave up on avoiding the draft and enlisted in the Marine Corps where he was well received. I guess the marines are used to fellows like Joe Brody. My mother could always make him behave. He became a platoon commander up near the DMZ and wrote letters about the carnage. "The Officers Club was fragged. Fortunately I was around back smoking a joint. There was blood all over the place."

"There was blood all over the place!" Karen shouted over the telephone, long distance, collect. After four years studying fashion at the two-year college downtown she had transferred to Kent State and was running around and squealing fashionably with the rest of the demonstrators when the National Guard shot at them. Karen was getting a knack for being onsite when things were going to hell. She was unscathed. Kent State was closed. Karen came east to "join the movement."

All the colleges in Ohio were closed. Jim Fisk was working on his MA in political science at Selective State (thesis topic: "Indomitable Trends in American Politics: The Vision of Senator Eugene McCarthy"). He visited me too. We had a private moment, around the corner from the shabby row house where *Puddles* had its office, drinking beer at the Ebony Lounge where the *Puddles* staff was tolerated because we drank a lot of beer.

"Who goes to Kent State?" said Jim.

"Um . . . ," I said (this was before the world knew that Michael Keaton, Drew Carey, and most of Devo were Kent State alumni), "kids whose families aren't that well-off, kids who kind of scraped through high school, kids who are avoiding the draft."

"Who joins the National Guard?"

"Kids whose families aren't that well-off, kids who kind of scraped through . . ."

"We just shot ourselves," said Jim.

There was an enormous, angry demonstration at Ivy Wannabe. We considered Kent State an earth-shattering event. College students were being damaged. The Earth Day demonstration two weeks before had attracted maybe a hundred people.

Karen, in her capacity as outraged eyewitness, addressed the crowd inexpertly and at length through a bullhorn. I was proud of her, but with a feeling I couldn't describe at the time. Now, having spent the requisite years listening to my children at recitals, recitations, thespian performances, and speeches to school assemblies, I know what I was thinking. This isn't making any goddamned sense and when the fuck will it be over.

I dodged the draft with the help of a former captain in the Army Medical Corps who'd become a hippie, wrote a health advice column for *Puddles* called "HIPpocratic Oath," and ran a free clinic that mostly treated crab lice. He composed a long letter for me to take to my draft physical. It outlined my deep-seated psychiatric problems:

- makes careless mistakes in schoolwork
- does not seem to listen
- is often easily distracted
- fidgets with hands or feet or squirms in seat
- runs about or climbs excessively
- has difficulty playing or engaging in leisure activities quietly

And it contained four pages about my history of drug abuse, three and a half of them devoted to listing the drugs I'd abused. "You don't need to *act* like a lunatic," the hippie doctor advised.

I carried the document in a fat manila envelope. My fellow recipients of a "Greetings" and I were transported by bus to the draft induction center at some ungodly hour like 9 a.m. There we were assembled in a large room standing in rows in our socks and underwear. All the guys wearing Gold Toe over-the-calf length men's dress socks and boxer shorts were holding fat manila envelopes. All the guys wearing the kind of socks that are bought by the bagful at Kmart and Y-front Hanes underpants that come up over your belly button were not.

I suppose I should have noticed that the bourgeois pigs were hogging the fat manila envelopes. But getting drafted was an earth-shattering event. And the problem with belonging to a generation that always speaks personally is that everything comes down to a first-person story. I admire junior Baby Boomer Jay McInerney's attempt, in his book *Bright Lights,*

Big City, to use the second-person voice. But enough about you, Jay.

The army doctor in charge of the draft physical sent me to the army psychiatrist in charge of people with fat manila envelopes. The psychiatrist, as he was reading the letter I'd given him while I was being easily distracted and fidgeting in my seat, began to back his chair away from mine. When he'd finished the letter he said, "Ah-hem. Do you still take drugs?"

I did not seem to listen. Finally I said, "I'm really not into drugs anymore at all, man. I mean, like, I smoke grass. But that's herbal. Like a all-natural thing. But I'm really not into drugs. I mean if I'm tired or something I might do some speed. You know, to keep me going and everything. And if I sort of start freaking out on the speed I'll do some downers or get a bottle of Robitussin. Smack's not my thing, man. You get all strung out on smack. I drop acid. Like when things get heavy. Acid trips give you this groovy perspective. I mean, like mescaline and peyote. Peyote is a real trip. But I'm really not into drugs anymore at all. Although I do drink a lot."

By this time the psychiatrist was standing up behind his chair, with the chair between him and me. He was getting red in the face.

"Do you have a home?!"

"I, like, crash at places."

"What do you do for a living?!"

"I'm totally into it. Like, you know, living."

"Do you know why you're here?!"

"Oh, wow, that's heavy, man."

"You're fucked up!" the psychiatrist said. (Are psychiatrists allowed to say things like that? Or only army psychiatrists? I'll have to ask Al Bartz. Anyway, this interchange at the draft physical casts some doubt on the idea that the Baby Boom is the Therapeutic Generation.)

"You don't belong in the army!" the psychiatrist said. "You need help!"

I couldn't help that Karen moved in with me although I was already living with another girlfriend, who actually did call herself something like Sunshine, in this case Windflower. And she was missing some of her petals. Before any carnal images, bygone fantasies, or false memories from long ago are aroused in the minds of my fellow male Baby Boomers, let me say that the leaders of the Taliban, Al-Qaeda, and such-like are ensconced in households with multiple mates and that there is nothing SEAL Team Six can do to them that is worse than what's going on at home.

We all lived in the *Puddles* row house. *Puddles*, like many such publications around the country, called itself an "underground newspaper" because that's what *Combat*, the clandestine publication of the French Resistance during World War II, was called. *Combat* was edited by Albert Camus and Jean-Paul Sartre. *Puddles* was edited by Hairy Bob and me. *Combat* was in constant danger of being raided by the Gestapo seeking vicious reprisals. *Puddles* was in occasional danger of being raided by the police seeking small amounts of marijuana.

Puddles was named *Puddles* because nobody could figure out what to name it. At the time Hairy Bob started the newspaper he had a girlfriend with a four-year-old son. The son had a puppy named Puddles. The name of the dog was considered hilarious by the boy, who went around the house repeating it over and over.

The *Puddles* staff consisted of Hairy Bob, me, Wind-flower, Karen, Skinny Bob who was a student at Ivy Wannabe's journalism school and would become a real newspaper reporter someday and already owned a trench coat, and the staff photographer, Hairy Bob's best friend, Steverino Leary. Plus there were a number of wanderers in and hangers around supplying unpaid articles and artwork and unpaid labor getting the layout together for the latest issue, whenever we got it together to have a latest issue.

Not that we got paid ourselves. When we were broke we would go downtown and stand on the sidewalk and sell the papers ourselves for 25 cents. It was surprising how many people would give Hairy Bob, who had large goggling eyes and was quite untidy, a quarter just because he was standing there yelling "Puddles!" Often they didn't even take the paper. And then we would go to the Ebony Lounge.

For a publication that included a lot of long bourgeois pig rants, *Puddles* was good-natured. We printed the *Fabulous Furry Freak Brothers* comic strip by Gilbert Shelton on the front page. (And, Gilbert, if you're still looking for the syndication fees, I live in, um, Auckland.) We ran personal ads that provided amusement. "Happening older dude seeking out-of-sight chick for blind date." The doctor was funny in his "HIPpocratic Oath" column.

> *Q. When I get really stoned I think there's something large and horrible in the attic.*
> *A. Buy a hook and eye latch, attach it to the attic door, and make sure it's fastened before you take drugs.*

After the police raided the *Puddles* office seeking small amounts of marijuana, *Puddles* ran a photograph of the office in a state of extreme mess, captioned, "*Puddles* office after police drug search." Under which was the same photograph captioned, "*Puddles* office before police drug search."

When waterbeds came on the market in 1971 we conducted extensive testing. We conducted very extensive testing. It's a wonder the second floor of the *Puddles* row house withstood our published findings. I doubt the contents of *Combat* were presented with as light a touch.

Steverino Leary was something of a misfit at *Puddles*. This was a time when many Baby Boomers were eagerly pursuing the label of misfit, but some of us fitted into being misfits better than others. Steverino had creases in his bell-bottoms. And he was ahead of the 1970s curve with lime green and canary yellow shirts, some of which had ruffles. "My wife likes to iron," he said. An alarming statement even before Gloria Steinem had published the first issue of *Ms*. We never saw his wife.

Steverino spent nearly all his time at the *Puddles* office, mostly with the wanderers in and hangers around, mostly with the cute girl ones. He said pot gave him a headache; he liked beer better. (Secretly, so did I. Pot made me sensitively perceptive and, what with Karen and Windflower in the same house and the sixties in general, I was beginning to wonder if sensitively perceptive was a good thing.) He said he was a bitterly disillusioned Vietnam vet. Well, not Vietnam exactly. He'd been in the navy and stationed in the Philippines, but we could dig what he was saying. We're a generation that sets great store by bitter disillusionment. Given our illusions, this has stood us in good stead. And Steverino wasn't quite as broke as the rest of us—"military disability"—and he had a camera and knew how to develop film.

Also Steverino had helped Hairy Bob and Skinny Bob and me harbor a fugitive on the run, Larry I'm-Not-Telling-You-My-Real-Name, as he called himself. He was not on the run from the law. Real Name Larry, as we called him, was on the run from the Weathermen or the Weather Underground or whatever they were calling themselves at the moment. The moment being a couple days after March 6, 1970, when members of the New York Weathermen cell had blown themselves up while trying to make a bomb in the basement of a rich-girl cell member's parents' house on West Eleventh Street in Greenwich Village. It was what bomb squads refer to as a "self-criticizing exercise."

"Those motherfucking crazy motherfuckers are fucking crazy," said Real Name Larry. "They used to have 'ideological struggle,' which meant you sit around in a circle and everybody screams at each other, but now they've formed 'cells' and gone 'underground,' which means in some rich-girl cell member's parents' house when the parents are in Bermuda, and they lock themselves in the house and spend twenty hours a day 'struggling' about 'armed struggle' and 'white skin privilege.'"

I had never heard so many internal quotation marks in a single sentence and wouldn't again until irony flourished and air quotes bloomed.

"And," said Real Name Larry, "monogamy and fascio-hetro-sexualism have been abolished. Everybody's supposed to fuck everybody. Yuck."

I also had never heard those last two sentiments expressed in conjunction. They would prove prescient later in the newly fledged decade.

Real Name Larry had become interested in ideological struggle when he was a student at the University of Michigan at Flint. If you've ever been to Flint, you'll realize that almost anything that doesn't have to do with Flint can seem interesting there. We'd hidden him in the attic (hook and eye latch on the inside of the door). It took him three weeks to get up the nerve to go home and live with his mother.

Several months after Real Name Larry left we had an ideological struggle of our own. The *Puddles* office was invaded by a group of local radicals who called themselves the Balto-Cong. It's the one name of any consequence that I haven't changed in this book. How could it be improved?

The Balto-Cong believed in armed struggle and white skin privilege—that is to say they didn't believe in white skin privilege—and apparently we did or, in the matter of armed struggle, didn't. They came through the front door one evening waving sticks and fists and saying they were "liberating" the *Puddles* capitalist rip-off newspaper in the name of "The People."

Steverino was off somewhere, maybe with one of the cute girl wanderers in. Hairy Bob and Skinny Bob and Karen and Windflower and I were there. We tried to explain that the *Puddles* capitalist rip-off newspaper consisted, at that point, of a $3,000 debt owed to Hairy Bob's parents, $4,500 in unpaid printing bills, a house where the rent was three months overdue, and a couple of typewriters. Frankly, The People were welcome to it.

Instead we were held at stick- and fistpoint and subjected to consciousness raising. Consciousness raising is different from ideological struggle in that during ideological struggle you sit around in a circle and everybody screams at each other while during consciousness raising you sit in the middle of a circle and everybody screams at you. It resembles a certain kind of family gathering when you were a kid, if you were a certain kind of kid.

There were fifteen or eighteen Balto-Cong. Hairy Bob's eyes goggled and he did quite a bit of screaming back, as did Karen. The consciousness raising showed every sign of going on all night and might have done so if two of The People, who lived down the block, hadn't wandered in and scared the Balto-Cong away.

These were Philip and Levon, two good-sized young men sporting the currently fashionable leather-coat Huey P. Newton look. They were honor students at the local high school and often came to the *Puddles* office in hope that we would publish their poetry. And, after that evening, I'm glad to say we did.

"What the heck's going on here?" said Philip, the larger of the two. And the whole Balto-Cong contingent headed for the door.

Windflower, however, went with them. Her consciousness had been raised.

I have been told that, the next day, I went around the office banging my fist on things and yelling, "Spiro Agnew was right!"

The Balto-Cong could come back. We decided that somebody should be standing guard every night at the *Puddles* office. We didn't know anybody who got up before noon so we didn't worry about somebody standing guard all day. We stood guard faithfully for a week until we began to forget to. At the end of that week Steverino and I were standing guard although not very well because Steverino had brought a six-pack and we forgot to lock the front door.

For the purpose of standing guard, Steverino had his service automatic, which he'd tucked in the waistband of his creased bell-bottom pants between the ruffles of his canary yellow shirt. I had a .22 pistol, a gift from Uncle Mike. My pistol was in the drawer of the *Puddles* office front desk where Karen, when she felt like it, sat and asked people who wandered in or were hanging around if they had any articles or artwork that they wanted to not get paid for.

We had just come back from looking in the refrigerator to double-check that the six-pack was gone. Steverino was leaning against a wall and I was standing behind the desk and the front door banged open.

The Balto-Cong had come back. There were fifteen or eighteen of them again, quite a crowd in our modest entry-way. Steverino reached for his automatic, but in his alarm, and with some hindrance from ruffles, he shoved the gun down his trousers. I rushed to the desk, opened the desk drawer, stuck my hand inside, and grabbed the pistol. However, in my rush to the desk I had rushed right up against it, and once I had my hand around the pistol I couldn't get my hand out of the desk drawer because I couldn't open the desk drawer because my thigh was in the way.

Steverino thrust his hand into the front of his pants in search of the automatic. My gun and hand were stuck in the drawer. Steverino fumbled in his pants. I banged the gun around in the desk. The Balto-Cong were confronted by somebody wildly groping himself and somebody else whose arm was apparently being eaten by a desk drawer. It gave them pause.

I was thinking quick: "If I can't get the gun out of the drawer because I can't get the drawer open because my thigh is in the way, I'll slip the safety off, cock the hammer, and shoot through the desk." Just as I'd formed this plan the Balto-Cong crowd parted and there was Windflower.

Windflower seemed oblivious to Steverino and me but, then again, Windflower generally did seem oblivious. She announced, "I left my steam iron and my ironing board here."

As I said, the sixties produced various enigmas. What was Windflower, who wore nothing, and I mean nothing at all, but tie-dyed muumuus, doing with a steam iron and an ironing board? If Windflower was ironing her hair she was doing it about as well as I would my button-down dress shirts when I finally got a coat and tie and was a bachelor. And what did this have to do with Steverino's wife who liked to iron? There were no coincidences in the sixties. "Far out," I probably said. The Balto-Cong seemed to regard the situation as far out themselves. They hesitated by the front door.

Windflower marched upstairs. She marched back downstairs with an ironing board under her right arm and a Sunbeam steam iron in her left hand. Steverino gave up the search for the automatic. I uncocked the .22.

It's the only time I've ever pointed a gun at anyone. It looks better in the movies.

The youth gets together his materials to build a bridge to the moon . . . and, at length, the middle-aged man concludes to build a woodshed with them.

—Henry David Thoreau

16

REAL LIFE

Adulthood, however, pursues the most evasive grown-up. I got a job. I consulted the want ads. There wasn't anything under "incomprehensible poets" and no one was looking to hire bourgeois pig ranters. I got a job as a messenger. This was before the era of bicycle messengers, with their distinctive glamour. I took the bus. Occasionally I received a smile from a pretty receptionist until she realized what my occupation was.

I made $75 a week. Payday came every two weeks. I'd moved out of the *Puddles* office a couple of months before. I was looking forward to the $150 and so was my landlord. When I got my paycheck I found that I netted $82.27 after federal income tax, state income tax, city income tax, Social Security, union dues, and pension fund contribution.

I was a communist. I had protested for communism. I had demonstrated for communism. I had rioted for communism. Then I got a capitalist job and found out we had communism already.

I had long ago smashed up my motorcycle. While I was sprawled in the street, two cops in a patrol car stopped, called an ambulance, and hunched over me, trying to see how unconscious I'd been knocked. One cop asked, "Do you know your name? What year is it? Who's the president of the United States?"

I said, "Johnson, Nixon, one of those sons of bitches."

"Oh, he's okay," said the other cop.

Steverino Leary turned out to be a cop. Three protesters went on trial for smashing the windows in city hall and beaning a traffic policeman during a demonstration in favor of peace in Vietnam. Skinny Bob was covering—he was fond of using newspaper reporter words—the trial for *Puddles*. As evidence, the prosecutor presented the jury with several glossy photographs of the three protesters smashing the windows in city hall and beaning a traffic policeman.

Steverino had taken the photographs. Skinny Bob knew this because he and Hairy Bob and I had looked at the photographs Steverino took at the demonstration and had decided that several of them, involving smashing windows and beaning a traffic policeman, did not show peace protesters in their best light. We tore up the photos and flushed them down the toilet at the *Puddles* office, a prolonged process. The toilet always clogged.

Only one person could have developed a second set of those photographs. Meanwhile, this one person and Hairy

Bob were on a road trip to a pop festival in Atlanta that was almost as successful (Richie Havens played) as Woodstock. Midway to Atlanta Steverino confessed to his best friend that he was a plainclothes Baltimore police officer, working undercover at the *Puddles* office.

Maybe my reaction would have been, "You call those ruffles *plainclothes*?"

Or maybe, "In that case, when you finally fished the automatic out of the cuff of your bell-bottoms, why didn't you shoot some goddamn Balto-Cong?"

Or maybe not. I was still young.

Hairy Bob's reaction was bitter disillusionment. He made Steverino stop the car. Hairy Bob got out and hitchhiked home.

Skinny Bob got back to the *Puddles* office about an hour after Hairy Bob did. Skinny Bob was in tumult about his scoop. Hairy Bob was in tears about his friend.

Hairy Bob blubbered, "Steverino is a cop!"

"Steverino is a cop!" Skinny Bob exclaimed.

It turned out okay. We're a generation that doesn't appreciate consequences. And we appreciated consequences even less after the Vietnam War, which had 47,415 of them in combat, not counting 153,303 wounded. At the end of the 1970s there was a catchphrase, "Don't sweat the small stuff . . . And it's all small stuff," always spoken more in hope than expectation. (Richard Carlson, the Baby Boomer psychotherapist who turned the catchphrase into a best seller in 1997, died while on book tour, the consequence of a pulmonary embolism.)

Steverino really did consider Hairy Bob to be his best friend. When it came time for him to testify at the protesters' trial he claimed he couldn't identify them because "my view was blocked by the camera." The protesters got off. The beaned traffic policeman recovered.

A year later Hairy Bob ran into Steverino at the Ebony Lounge. Hairy Bob refused Steverino's offer to buy him a beer. Twice. I wasn't there so I don't know exactly how the conversation went. Steverino bought Hairy Bob a beer on the third try.

Hairy Bob said that Steverino wasn't a bitterly disillusioned Vietnam vet. He joined the police force to avoid being drafted. They assigned him to go undercover because he owned bell-bottom pants. He was supposed to infiltrate *Puddles* and spy on dangerous radicals, but we weren't ones, and he liked us, and we became his friends, and it was a great way to meet cute hippie girls. His wife did like to iron. And he had refused to testify against the peace protesters.

"Steverino is back in uniform," Hairy Bob said, "riding in a patrol car."

Which, now that year-round mugging by heroin addicts was replacing summer riots, the city could use some more of, as far as I was concerned.

"What about spying on the goddamned Balto-Cong?" I asked.

"Steverino said the only dangerous radical thing they ever did was take over the *Puddles* office."

The political, cultural, and social phenomena of the sixties became a thin film spreading to everywhere in the 1970s, a shiny, multicolored iridescence that was beautiful to behold in a certain light. Like the slick from the Torrey Canyon oil spill. Call us a superficial and slippery generation if you will, but

Pliny the Elder, Plutarch, the Venerable Bede, and Benjamin Franklin all make positive mention of "pouring oil on troubled waters." Nonetheless some cleaning up was required.

Hairy Bob, heedless of my grandmother, became a Democrat. Others of us became otherwise. Some got the memo late. Real Name Larry's motherfucking crazy motherfucker Weathermen went on bombing things—U.S. Capitol men's room, Pentagon women's room, various other rooms in government offices, police precincts, and corporate headquarters. Not many innocent lives were lost. Intentionally, it is claimed. Inexpertly, it is suspected.

I happened to be in, or at, one of the worst of the 1970s bombings, on December 29, 1975, at LaGuardia Airport. I don't think the Weathermen did it. I don't think anyone has ever figured out who did it, but it was somebody who thought he was such a big ideological left-winger, I'll bet. Karen had returned to Ohio. I was flying to Cleveland to see her. For once she wasn't right there when things were going to hell, if you don't count what happened to Cleveland in the 1970s.

A bomb equivalent in size to twenty-five sticks of Uncle Mike's hayfield dynamite went off on the arrivals level. Pieces of bodies were strewn across LaGuardia's lower roadway. It is the opinion of the Baby Boom that no other generation has ever felt the horror of strewn pieces of bodies as acutely as the Baby Boom. I got letters from Joe Brody, when he was still in Vietnam, about leading his platoon into Vietnamese villages that had been bombed. He expressed the same opinion about the callous nature ("asshole shithead fuckwads" was the way he put it) of his senior officers.

I was upstairs on the departures level when the bomb went off. I was in the concourse bar and had just ordered a drink from the bartender, a guy about my age wearing a gunfighter mustache. There was an immense shock and crash. We didn't know if was a bomb or if an airplane had crashed into the terminal, but some terrible event had taken place. We Baby Boomers are sensitive to these things. "Make that a double?" said the bartender.

If Steverino Leary got valuable information about the Weathermen out of Real Name Larry it didn't do much to aid the authorities. You can't make a joke out of terrorism, especially now that globalization has produced a larger, cheaper, more efficient international terrorizing supply chain. But I'm glad we've outsourced most of it. Wherever the motherfucking crazy motherfucker militant Islamic fundamentalists are, at least I'm not hiding them in the *Puddles* attic.

Weathermen leaders Bernardine Dohrn and Bill Ayers never were captured. They had to turn themselves in, in 1980. Now they're passing acquaintances of the president of the United States. Some say this is dim of the president. Some say this is hypocritical of Bernardine and Bill. But, in the far reaches of our hearts, we, with our deep Baby Boom dislike of the consequential, say, "Is this a great country or what?"

Skinny Bob, who did become a newspaper reporter, used the Freedom of Information Act to get a copy of the Baltimore Police Department file on *Puddles*.

When the police had raided the *Puddles* office seeking— and finding—small amounts of marijuana, the charges were soon dropped. According to the file, "Officer [redacted] recommends that drug possession arrests be nol pros to avoid jeopardization of undercover status of Officer [redacted] at premises at which drug possession search warrant had been issued upon." Personal information in the files included such items as "*Puddles* staff member [redacted] states his opposition to prejudice, poverty, war, and injustice. In the opinion of undercover Police Officer [redacted], staff member [redacted]'s motivation is to annoy his parents."

The Baby Boom starts to produce rather than consume American culture when we get to be in our late twenties—about the same age I was when I saw a sidelong reflection in the window of a storefront bay and, not realizing I was looking at myself, thought, "That guy is getting a little old for the embroidered work shirt, frayed jeans, and barbers-on-strike look."

Speaking of twenties, let me apologize for what I said, fourteen chapters ago, about the twenties being a failed experiment at having a sixties. The sixties was a failed experiment at having a sixties. Think how things would be if they'd turned out the way, for a moment, they looked like they might—a February Sunday spent in Dirty Eddie's unheated geodesic dome eating macrobiotic brown rice and drinking Mu tea while watching Hacky Sack Super Bowl VIII.

The Baby Boom's influence, as opposed to existence, begins to matter in 1974. Younger Baby Boomers are mostly in high school and junior high. The very youngest are ten and thus approaching the mental age for which our generation is famous. Older Baby Boomers have finally cleared the bongs and empty Mallomar boxes out of the finished basement at my house. Bill Clinton is running for Congress, so there's ample sexual tension, a key component of Baby Boom life. Stephen King (born 1947) publishes *Carrie*. Steven Spielberg (born 1946) makes his big-screen debut, *The Sugarland Express*, with its eerie prefiguring of the highway pursuit of O. J. Simpson (born 1947). And Spielberg is working on something that will demolish the intellectual pretensions of an entire art form—*Jaws*, the movie that destroyed cinema.

Demolishing pretensions is a hallmark of the Baby Boom. Note the lack of artistic pretensions, or art, in the 1974 recording of "Hey Joe" by Patti Smith (born 1946). This is supposedly the first example of punk rock. Uncoincidentally, the same year, "Rock the Boat" is the first example of disco to hit number 1 on the pop charts. *National Lampoon*'s circulation peaks. And what will become *Saturday Night Live* is being planned at 30 Rock. The irony pandemic has begun.

Some aspects of a Baby Boom world are not yet evident. Bill Gates is still cutting classes at Harvard. Steve Jobs is knocking around India looking for transcendental iPhone apps. But Pong machines are showing up in bars. The long night of electronic "Roamin' in the Gloamin'" is beginning to fall.

And the Baby Boom's politics are beginning to take form, of which there is none aside from Middle-class Resentment. Once being big ideological left-wingers blew up in our faces we were hopelessly split. One could consult the polling data on this subject. But a generation that is expert at lying to ourselves isn't going to have trouble pulling George Gallup's leg. The first thing that happened after the Twenty-sixth Amendment lowered the voting age to eighteen was a landslide victory by Richard Nixon.

Baby Boomers who are younger or female tend to vote for the Silly Party. Baby Boomers who are older or male tend to vote for the Stupid Party. Then there are the Independents, proud of the fact that they don't know which is which. The Baby Boomer presidents that we've had so far—Bill Clinton,

George W. Bush, and Barack Obama—are spread as far across the political map as you can get without going to Pyongyang.

Sometime around 1974 I actually did read a little Karl Marx. Karl was a bit of a Baby Boomer before the fact—middle-class attorney's son, sometimes sudent radical, unpublished novelist and poet, "underground" journalist, sponger on a crackpot rich buddy, and talking through his hat. Karl Marx was a very smart man. *Das Kapital* is a very bad hat.

Given all the liberties the Baby Boom has taken, we ought to be libertarian. We should be adhering to the "Clinton Rules." That is to say, the rules the Clintons exemplified: Mind your own business, and keep your hands to yourself. Hillary, mind your own business. Bill, keep your hands to yourself.

But the libertarian creed of individual dignity, individual liberty, and individual responsibility comes with that responsibility kicker. And there's the *Atlas Shrugged* doorstop, which got some Baby Boomers all excited and the rest of us wondering who hid the Strunk and White. Plus a wholehearted embrace of Ayn Rand's philosophy of dimly lit enlightened self-interest can end up making somebody sound like a selfish, loony old bitch such as Ayn Rand. Better if we all just claim we're "a social liberal and a fiscal conservative." And never mind what the farm boy said when he saw the circus giraffe. There ain't no such creature.

What we actually are is antinomian. It's a theological doctrine. The Baby Boom is not a generation much given to studying theology. But we seem to have figured out this one. Antinomianism is the belief that faith (the Baby Boom has a lot of faith—in itself) and grace (the Baby Boom has been graced with a lot of good things) allow men (and, let us hasten to add, women) to be (according to *Webster's Third International*) "freed not only from the Old Testament law of Moses and all forms of legalism but also from all law including the generally accepted standards of morality prevailing in any given culture." That's us in a nutshell.

For a term used by theologians, *antinomian* is unusually clear-cut: Latin *anti-* "against" Greek *nomos* "the law." Antinomianism was carried to an extreme by the third-century gnostic Christian sect known as Ophites. (*Gnostic* is another good Baby Boom word, from the Greek "know-it-all.") The Ophites revered Cain, the Sodomites, and the Genesis serpent and thought that the good guy in Exodus was the pharaoh. That's us when we're carrying things to extremes. We're a generation that is often accused of carrying things to extremes. In fact we're a generation that carries things as far as we want to, until we get tired of carrying them, then we drop them on the rest of you. But we've never dropped our antinomianism. "No Rules" is the motto of a popular Baby Boom steak house chain.

It may seem to be a contradiction that a generation opposed to personal restrictions of any kind has, since coming into political power, created a welter of legal and regulatory intrusions on private life. My kids have to wear hockey helmets to play puff billiards. But we're a contradictory generation.

And it's fun to make rules—for other people. Our spouses would kill us if they caught us with a Big Gulp, we gave up smoking, and we're fifty-plus, so what do we care about 64-ounce Mountain Dews, lighting up within 10,000 feet of a building entrance, and not being able to buy a beer even though you're old enough to vote, get married, fight in Afghanistan, and be executed by lethal injection? And too bad about people who have to take their shoes off at airports because they aren't flying private.

Besides, it's the job of politicians to pass laws. And the Baby Boom is very good at politics. We've vaulted the threshold. We've mastered the skill set. We have the enormous power of bullshit, using bullshit in the political science sense, as a technical term meaning "political science."

Other generations say Baby Boom politics are polarized. Don't they know their history? What's happened to the American educational system? (I mean, other than that we took it over?) Now, 1861—that was polarized. MoveOn.Org? Tea Party? We have game on. We've got tremendous depth of bench. The point spread is zero. We came to play. We're *great* at politics. Other generations are just jealous. We're so good they can't forgive us.

"I can't forgive myself," said Joe Brody. It was sometime in the late 1970s. I was at his house out in the woods in New Hampshire. It was late at night. Joe's kids and wife were in bed. We'd had too much to drink. Joe said, "I can't forgive myself for what I did in Vietnam." And he began to cry.

And I thought, "Oh, Christ."

It was only a few years since Lieutenant Calley, given life in prison for the My Lai massacre, had had his sentence commuted by Richard Nixon. I didn't want to come off as less sensitive and understanding than Richard Nixon, but . . .

We needed more to drink. "Joe," I said, "we've known each other for twenty years. Whatever happened, I understand."

Joe said, "It was my second tour. I had this platoon, all draftees. I mean by then any idiot could figure out a way to dodge the draft."

"I understand."

"Every day when we'd go out on patrol we'd just go out. I'm so ashamed of what happened."

"What happened?"

"We'd just go out."

"I don't understand."

"I hid them. We'd go out on patrol, and as soon as we were far enough away I'd stick everybody behind a dike in some rice paddy, and we'd sit there smoking cigarettes and listening to Sly and the Family Stone on the ghetto blaster, and when we came back I'd lie about all the hooches we'd searched and bad guys we'd had firefights with. I'm a marine, damn it. I don't know if I can ever forgive myself."

If I'd been thinking quick, I would have said, "If Henry Kissinger can forgive himself for getting the Nobel Peace Prize, your ass is golden."

. . . . that desire to do good without too much
personal inconvenience that lurks in most of us.
—Barbara Pym,
The Sweet Dove Died

17

RIPENESS IS ALL

Everything's all right. It turned out okay. Better than okay. Life has been much more fun since the Baby Boom took over. "Mommy, why are there scarves tied to the bedposts in Daddy's and your bedroom?" And there are plenty of fun tales to be told about the Baby Boom in the 1980s, the '90s, the '00s, and today. But we're saving them for psychotherapy sessions. If you go to a psychotherapy session and just sit there saying nothing it makes it seem like something's wrong with you, psychologically.

By the end of the 1970s the Baby Boom character had been formed. Our last youthful exuberance, "Punk," came just before Generation X's first youthful exuberance, "Goth"—a subtle shift from "fuck you" to "I'm fucked" that indicates the Baby Boom will remain in control for a long time to come.

Our passionate belief in change hasn't altered, going from "spare change?" to "Hope and Change" with stops along the way for "you'd better change your ways," "change of life," and "any change in a wart or mole."

We're still opposed to prejudice, poverty, war, and injustice —when they happen to us. But at least we're opposed to them. There have been times and places—the 1960s South, Benedictine monasteries, the 1860s South, and divorce court—where previous generations made strong arguments in favor of the aforementioned, which you won't hear us doing. At least not very often except in divorce court or during hostile corporate takeovers or when Iran has nuclear weapons or looks like it maybe does or wants to.

If the Baby Boom went around being prejudiced against races, religions, ethnic groups, genders, and sexual orientations, date night would be pretty much down to a dose of Cialis and a box of tissues on the bedside table.

Who would invest in our BabyBoondoggle IPO if poverty meant nobody had enough money to buy the worthless stock?

War is wrong—itchy uniforms and ugly shoes.

We don't like injustice. We don't like justice either. Because we're the generation that's *not judgmental*. And who the hell put traffic surveillance cameras at every goddamned intersection? (Oops. That was us. We put surveillance cameras everywhere when we remembered how Joe Brody and Billy and Bobby Stumf and Johnny MacKay and Steve Penske and Jerry Harris and I were going to vandalize North Side High's football field with weed killer.)

*   *   *

The Baby Boom has had politics figured out since at least 1980. An American and a Russian are talking about Ronald Reagan and Leonid Brezhnev. The American says, "I hate Reagan so much I pissed on his limousine." The Russian says, "I hate Brezhnev so much I *shit* on his limousine." The American says, "Well, to tell the truth, Reagan wasn't in the limousine when I pissed on it." The Russian says, "Well, to tell the truth, my pants weren't down."

The key is inept leadership. This makes things easy on followers. The Baby Boom has always gone in for following inept leaders. Follow Keith Richards and you can wind up in some sort of trouble. Follow Napoleon and you can wind up in Moscow.

Prior generations didn't have politics figured out. When my godmother was a freshman in high school she began to read the *Atlantic Monthly* in the school library. One night at dinner she announced, "I think Coolidge is a dope." Her father made her stand in the front hall closet for half an hour for showing disrespect to the president of the United States. I have it on good authority that President Reagan told the limousine joke himself.

Prior generations didn't have diversity figured out either. There was another joke, considered quite hip in 1962, and the laugh line was almost the same as what the serious pundits were saying about who was most likely to be elected president in 2008. A man dies and goes to heaven but doctors resuscitate him and he comes back to life and everybody wants to know what's God like. "She's black."

Being different wasn't always considered normal, if not obligatory. Not even in the freewheeling sixties. When Tim Minsky was a senior at Yale he shared an off-campus apartment with a roommate who was diabetic. This was before the ready availability of disposable needles and the roommate was supposed to boil his syringe after every insulin injection. One of the kids with whom Tim and I had gone to high school, a serious type named Danny Phelps, was applying to grad school at Yale and stopped by to visit Tim. Danny glanced into the pot of water boiling on the stove and gave Tim a puzzled look.

Tim said, "Danny, there's a confession I've been wanting to make for a long time. I've never told this to anyone. I'm a heroin addict."

Danny sat down at the kitchen table, burst into tears, and said, "Tim, there's a confession I've been wanting to make for a long time. I've never told this to anyone. I'm a homosexual."

If Tim had been thinking quick he would have said, "So's Anderson Cooper and Barney Frank and Rufus Wainwright and Alexander the Great and Gomer Pyle and the mutant superhero Northstar in Marvel Comics' X-Men (a perfect Baby Boom touch—identity politics for secret identities). But Tim couldn't think that quick because none of those people were out of the closet in 1968. Tim didn't know what to say and felt like a jerk.

And feminism is so far along among Baby Boomers that women aren't even bothering to make men feel like jerks anymore, outside of marriage. As far as I can tell "third wave feminists" are having a screaming senseless argument with themselves about whether women can be simultaneously managing director of the International Monetary Fund, chancellor of Germany, Nobel laureate, Supreme Court justice, author of the best-selling book series in history, CEO of Xerox, and mother of three when there are only so many hours in the day. I understand that House Minority leader Nancy Pelosi is lobbying Congress to lengthen the day to seventy-two hours. Meanwhile Baby Boom men are left to wonder (but never aloud) whether—hand that rocks the cradle and all that—feminism hasn't always been a matter of women having a leg wrestling match with their own other leg.

There are some things the Baby Boom has done that we're not proud of. We used up all the weird. It has always been the special prerogative of youth to look and act strange, to alarm and surprise their elders with peculiar dress and manners. Cicero mentioned it. "O tempora! O mores!" So did my mom, although in English. But the Baby Boom exhausted the available supply of peculiar. Weird clothes, we wore them. Weird beards, we grew them. Weird words and phrases, we said them. Weird attitudes, we had them. Thus when it came time for the next generation to alarm and surprise us with their peculiarities they were compelled to pierce their extremities and permanently ink their exposed flesh. That must have hurt. We apologize.

The Baby Boom unleashed the safety hysteria on the world. I recently bought a stepladder so festooned with stickers warning of the types and kinds of peril entailed in operating this device that it lacked only bold capital letters stenciled in signal orange upon each stepladder step: DO NOT STEP ON LADDER.

I cannot get into my car without setting off a panic among admonitory bells and buzzers cautioning me to buckle this, close that, and lock the other thing.

Of course each child must be accompanied by a full-scale parental security detail on every visit to a sporting event, school activity, shopping mall, public restroom, Scout jamboree, and Catholic Mass, especially if the tyke is within inappropriate touching distance of a priest or Scoutmaster.

We bother and control our older children and interfere in every aspect of their lives because we don't want them horning in on the fun of being juvenile, which rightfully belongs in perpetuity to the Baby Boom. Although I also blame the kids. In "The Helicopter Parent/Air-Support Child" relationship, it takes two to "Tango Hotel Papa to Alpha Sierra Charlie: debit card deposit in-bound at zero-nine hundred hours."

And despite the fact that we are now at the age when our generation has full control of the levers and pulleys of the American political mechanism, we haven't done much to legalize drugs except print up some "Medical Marijuana Makes Me Sick" bumper stickers.

"Safety" is so inconsistent with the spirit of the Baby Boom that it's like hearing the Clash performing Gilbert and Sullivan at the Nixon Library. Perhaps post-traumatic stress disorder explains the Baby Boom's safety hysteria. Doing the things our generation did and coming through them safely—that's hysterical.

Anyway, we grew up. We got married. We found true love. This wrecked the marriage. But we're a caring generation. We sometimes take care of the kids on weekends.

We got jobs. We made money. We spent it on cocaine. Then we made money with junk bonds for leveraged buyouts. Until the LBO market collapsed and the Savings and Loan crisis happened and some of us such as Michael Milken had to go to jail. Then we made money in the dot.com bubble. Hope you're not still waiting for the Webvan grocery delivery or the chew toy you ordered from Pets.com. Then we made money with subprime mortgage lending securitization and collateralized debt obligations. Sorry about the foreclosure. One thing about moving the family back to mom's house, she may be getting a little dotty but she still makes a great meat loaf. Now we'll make money with category-killer smartphone apps.

But whatever it is that the Baby Boom has and hasn't done, it's worked.

First, look at the butcher's bill. When the Greatest Generation took charge of America in 1961, their esteemed John F. Kennedy and his pals began a war that, according to the Department of Defense, left some 58,200 Americans dead from battle and its attendant accidents, incidents, and disease. And this for a purpose that has yet to be explained.

That's not as completely horrible as what the Idiot Generation preceding the Greatest Generation did. They killed 405,399 Americans in World War II and another 36,576 in the Korean War. True, the idiots didn't start the wars, but they did fuck-all to prevent or preempt them, and may they rot in hell.

The Baby Boom took charge of America (and hence, for all intents and purposes, the world) in 1988. That's when we decided to skip a generation of political leadership. We bypassed the ever risible Silent Generation represented by bobblehead Michael Dukakis trying to take a ride in a tank. (Younger readers should consult YouTube—a laugh is guaranteed.) We elected, as a sort of stand-in father figure, George H. W. Bush. And soon we'd have a Bill Clinton White House full of the Baby Boom and a Newt Gingrich Congress equally full of it.

Three hundred and eighty-two Americans died in the Persian Gulf War, 4,488 in the Iraq War, and 2,170 in Afghanistan as of this writing. That's an improvement. We do have blood on our hands. But there will be less "Out, damned spot! out, I say!" when our conscience performs its Act V of *Macbeth*. Although let us not let ourselves off too easily. What with allowing villainous slaughter to run amok in the Balkans for most of a decade, staying seated in the bleachers during the Rwanda butchery, being perfectly oblivious to the oncoming catastrophic attack on New York and Washington by militant Islamic fundamentalists, giving no thought to what the Pandora's box of the Iraq War contained for Iraqi civilians, and so on, we'll probably rot in hell, too, but in an upscale neighborhood of it.

Now look at the balance sheet. The size of the world economy has more than tripled since Baby Boom students quit paying attention in Economics class. World trade has grown enormously. I don't want to take all the credit myself, but I did buy a cheap Indian batik bedspread after I got my first job. The per capita gross domestic product of India, in 2013 dollars, was $691 in 1972 and is $1,734 now. Then I bought some cheap Japanese stereo equipment. Japan's per capita GDP went from $5,104 to $47,783 in the same period. Chinese electronics were even cheaper. China's per capita GDP has gone from $724 to $6,741. And we haven't done so badly ourselves with U.S. per capita GDP growing by $18,725 to reach a current figure of $51,248 on the Baby Boom's watch.

More to the point, morally speaking, there's the World Bank's index of global extreme poverty. By which they do mean extreme—people living on less than $1.25 a day. You can't even buy anything at the Dollar Store for $1.25 these days. In 1981, 52 percent of people in the developing world were that poor. By 1990 it was 43 percent. By 2008 (the last year for which the World Bank has complete data) it was 22 percent. This still leaves 1.29 billion people in starving and ragged misery. You might want to move the decimal point one place to the right on your check to Save the Children. But World Bank preliminary estimates indicate that, despite a worldwide economic slowdown, extreme poverty continues to abate.

The Baby Boom is more famous for repeatedly declaring that we're moral than for repeatedly acting that way, but the earth's increase in widespread well-being and decrease in widespread war couldn't have happened without a generation of self-indulgent Americans avid for all the good things in life and disinclined to put themselves—and hence, for all intents and purposes, the world—to too much trouble.

There have been some glitches in the Baby Boom's beneficent self-indulgence, especially when we were young and impetuous. The murder rate per 100,000 Americans went from 5.1 in 1960 when Joe Brody was first considering whacking his stepfather to 10.2 in 1980 when the Baby Boom was between sixteen and thirty-four and still buying blow and quaaludes from shady characters in the disco parking lot. We've gotten a grip on ourselves since then (and put a trigger lock on the pistol in the desk drawer). The murder rate is back to where it was in the halcyon 1950s.

We've had a generational tendency to "liberate" things going all the way back to Mrs. Furstein's decorative garden rocks. Incidence of property crime—burglaries, larcenies, and petty thefts—was at a rate of 1,534.3 per 100,000 in

1960. The rate was 3,309.0 by 1971. I assume the .0 represents Steverino Leary's failure to file a police report about the liberation of the *Puddles* office by the Balto-Cong. The rate peaked in 1980 at 4,851.1 and is now down to 2,703.1 although I don't know if Bear Stearns, Lehman Brothers, and Fannie Mae are counted in that figure.

And we always stole a lot of cars. At the time Joe Brody claimed he'd perpetrated theft-by-taking with the family automobile, the rate per 100,000 was already 183.0 and by 1989 it had reached 630.4. But that was during the "Bush Recession" just after we'd all splurged on BMWs, and how many of us parked them in a bad part of town with the windows down, took the bus home, and called Allstate?

A more persistent problem with the Baby Boom's beneficence is that we aren't as good as we claim we mean to be at spreading the benefits around. Although America's per capita wealth is 37 percent greater than it was when the Baby Boom began its rise to national domination, 15.1 percent of American families are now living below the official federal poverty level. In 1972 the percentage was 11.9.

This is not the World Bank's "extreme poverty." The U.S. government 2013 poverty threshold for a family of four is $23,550, food stamps, Medicaid, and housing subsidies not included. In 1950 dollars $23,550 would have been $2,436.43 or a weekly wage of $46.85. According to *Historical Statistics of the United States*, the average weekly salary of people employed in "finance, insurance, and real estate" was $50.52 in 1950, and the average salary of people in "retail trade" was $39.71.

If you're poor in America today you're making a little less than Billy and Bobby Stumf's dad was making selling whole life and term before his reserve unit got called up and he went off to fight in Korea for peanuts. And you're making a little more than Jerry Harris's dad was making managing the produce department at a grocery store.

But wherever we draw the poverty line, having 15.1 percent of the country below it is nothing to be complimented upon. And before we Baby Boomers indulge ourselves in some canned indignation about the gross inequities of corporate capitalism and how Warren Buffett's income tax rate is lower that his secretary's, let us pause to consider what our generation has left in its tracks. The fragile naifs who stayed at the sixties ball too long. The muddled goofs still beguiled by Large Thoughts. The drug-sodden burnouts. The poor souls who flunked their sexual license exams and were left with the illegitimate children and debilitating diseases. The way we failed to keep our eye on our sense of shame, which jumped bail and has been on the lam ever since. The swarm of divorces and slews of late and paltry child support payments. And the struggling immigrants who help us around the house and in the yard and whom we pay under the table and not damn much. It's a wonder 151 percent of the country isn't below the poverty line.

And yet we are the best generation in history. Which goes to show history stinks. But at least we are fabulous by historical standards.

The Baby Boom was a carefully conducted scientific experiment. The empirical results are us. Take the biggest generation in the most important country, put them in excessively happy families, give them too much affection, extravagant freedom, scant responsibility, plenty of money, a modicum of peace (if they dodged the draft), a profusion of opportunity, and a collapse of traditional social standards.

You get better people. Well, not *better*. Taken one by one, we're as maddeningly smug as Abel and as vile as Cain, the way people always have been. But we're better behaved. Although better behaved isn't the right way to put it either.

We're willful, careless, rash, vain, indulged, and entitled. We're "mad, bad, and dangerous to know," as Lady Caroline Lamb said of the poet, but she was an ex-girlfriend and ex-girlfriends say those things especially if you marry their cousin Annabella who had a few choice words about the poet herself, but she was an ex-wife and ex-wives say those things. The point here is that "a bunch of rhyme-less Lord Byrons" is a good description of the Baby Boom and the romantic, disorderly, harum-scarum lives we've led.

Except, of course, modern medicine cured the clubfoot, and we never slept with our sister—come on, there were plenty of other people to sleep with and it wasn't like we didn't have cars and couldn't get out of the house. And we haven't embarked on a campaign to liberate Greece. The EU has a central bank for that. Not that we didn't give the Greeks a few bucks to see the Parthenon and knock back some ouzos when we embarked on our Carnival cruise through the Aegean to Athens. And we didn't die of diarrhea at Missolonghi. The cruise ship gift shop had Imodium. Also our poetry is awful. The name Baby Boom poetry will be given in future literary anthologies is probably *worse libre*.

Other than that we're a lot like Lord Byron—larger than life personalities, providing the world with amusement, hearts in the right place even when our private parts aren't, thinking noble thoughts somewhat thoughtlessly, and being high-minded in a mindless sort of way.

We leave a mess behind, like Lord Byron did, but compare it to the mess that a generation previous left behind, like the generation previous to Lord Byron, which was Napoleon Bonaparte. You won't catch us—or George Gordon, 6th Baron, either—taking credit for plunging all of Europe into bloodshed by putting our own name on a bunch of wars or posing for pictures while groping ourselves with our hand someplace where there's nothing to grope or not leaving Moscow until it's on fire and it's winter and nobody has plowed the roads or letting the Battle of Waterloo be won on the playing fields of Eaton, which is nowhere near Belgium, or being the person everybody in the lunatic asylum is being. I mean, if I'm in the lunatic asylum, I'm just being me.

It's not a bad idea to have spoiled brats rule the world. The rulers of the ancient world may have been brats, but they weren't spoiled, if the Spartan mother admonishment to sons on their way to an all-guy outing—"Come back with your shield or on it"—is any indication.

Ancient potentates seemed to have had a firm sense of purpose rare among us pampered Baby Boomers eager for instant gratification. Mrs. Pharaoh must have popped her ankh when she caught Mr. Pharaoh blowing the IRA on a 455-foot Pyramid of Cheops for "his next stage in life." But he kept at it for twenty years. We'd never pull something like that, especially if our Queen of the Nile happened to be the principal breadwinner in the family and was already on the phone to the partner in her law firm who handles community property settlements.

And the mighty of yore must not have been doted upon sufficiently to make them emotionally needy and desirous of being liked by absolutely everybody. If Pontius Pilate had been a Baby Boomer, when he ordered the crucifixion he would have given Christ a "safe word."

Barbarian hordes used to run the ancient world too or, at any rate, run frequently into large parts of the ancient world to rape and pillage. The Baby Boom would make a lousy barbarian horde, no matter what Athenians had to say after we'd knocked back some ouzos. We'd be galloping across the Mongolian steppes sneezing because we're allergic to horse dander, going, "What, no sushi?" and living off the fat of the land when we're trying to cut down on the fat in our diet. Then it's time to rape and pillage. Rape is very wrong. Also it's damaging to the self-esteem. When somebody cries "Rape!" it's a rejection, not just of your actions and attitudes at the moment but of you as a whole person. Baby Boom barbarian horde members would be smiling shyly at the cowering womenfolk, asking, "Get pillaged often?" Then we'd start fiddling with the firebrand instead of burning the houses down and explain that we were trying to stop smoking. Plus pillaging means lugging all that stuff back with you before there were wheelie bags. And wheelie bags are probably hard to roll along the Mongolian steppes while you're galloping on a horse.

I don't think we would have been much use in the Middle Ages either, going on the Crusades by hitchhiking with flowers in our hair. Then we'd gather in a circle holding hands and try to levitate Jerusalem. If we'd had a be-in while Saladin was around I doubt he would have just let it be. We probably would have fared worse with the sultan in the Levant than we did with the National Guard at Kent State.

In fact, the Baby Boom wouldn't have been much good at committing any of history's atrocities, history being mostly a record of atrocities, and this may be why we got a D in it. Our generation would have discovered the New World, got a whiff of tobacco, said, "We can start smoking again!," moved in with the Indians, and convinced them to take their wigwams condo.

A Baby Boom Cortés, eyeing Montezuma, would have been thinking, "Gold? Nah. Got that hedged with long calls in precious metal commodities. How about an emerging market fund invested in outsourcing high-priced domestic Spanish Inquisition torture to low-cost overseas Aztec human sacrifice?"

The notorious triangle trade—sugar/rum/slaves—likewise would have been in Chapter 11 if operated by the Baby Boom. We use NutraSweet and Splenda. Rum means a Jimmy Buffett concert. And then we're so hungover we sleep right through the slave auction. Not that we ever would have brought Africans to America as human chattel. We would have brought Africans to America to make sure we never had to listen to "Turkey in the Straw" again.

History would have been very different—a C+ at least—if the Baby Boom had ruled the world.

And I will give children to be their princes, and babes shall rule over them.

—Isaiah 3:4

18

BIG DAMN MESSY BUNDLE OF JOY

And we will. Because the American Baby Boom is the future. We'll all turn into us eventually, as soon as families get excessively happy and start feeling too much affection for their kids. Unless, of course, extravagant freedom, scant responsibility, plenty of money, and a modicum of peace lead to such a high rate of carbon emissions that we all fry or drown. But you can't have everything. And you can have a profusion of opportunity and a collapse of traditional social standards.

Western Europe and the wealthiest parts of Asia and Latin America have had them already. And they're almost as useless as we are, meaning useless in the best abundant disposable income with ample leisure time to devote to pointless activities that don't harm anybody much except ourselves way.

Baby Boom–like places all seem to be engaged in bellicose national political deadlock the way we are in America. There's much tut-tutting about bellicose national political deadlock. But it's an improvement on bellicose national political purpose. World conquest, for example. "Mine eyes have seen the glory of the coming of the [insert name of deity or national leader whom you dislike most]/He is trampling out the vintage where the grapes of wrath are stored/He hath loosed the fateful lightning of his terrible swift sword . . ." That doesn't sound like any fun at all, except maybe the vintage trampling part.

We and our kindred generation of European Baby Boomers brought down the Berlin Wall. Reagan and Thatcher and Gorbachev get the kudos. But it was the Baby Boom that did the job.

After I'd given up on the messenger profession and become a foreign correspondent (you get the same frosty treatment from receptionists), I spent some time behind the Iron Curtain in the USSR, Poland, and East Germany. Everything, including the toilets, was made of crumbling concrete. Buildings were constructed without benefit of plumb bob or spirit level. There were wire mesh nets around the tops of the taller structures because pieces of the crumbling concrete kept falling off. Furniture looked as if it had been made by the seventh-grade shop class. Food was a lard sandwich except they were out of bread. Roads were paved with random bucketloads of asphalt dumped in the right-of-way. Cars, trucks, and buses had been reverse engineered from Tootsie Toys and went bumping down moon-cratered streets sputtering, misfiring, and burping clouds of smoke. You could have made a fortune standing on a Moscow street corner with a screwdriver and a timing light, had fortunes been allowed to be made.

"Cosmos" brand filter cigarettes had to be held upright or the tobacco dribbled out the end of the paper tube. Matches didn't work. After you struck a match you put it back in the matchbox because it was just as likely to light as any other match in there. The dial telephones buzzed with static. Assuming they were all tapped there must be reams of telephone conversation transcriptions somewhere in the KGB files reading: "zzzzzzz Nyet zzzzzzz Da zzzzzzz."

There was nothing to do but drink bad vodka and a lot of it. The Poles had a joke about a man from Warsaw who visits his brother in America. The brother says, "Would you like a drink?"

"Of course."

So the American brother goes to the liquor cabinet, gets out a bottle of vodka, and pours them both a drink.

"And then," says the man from Warsaw, "do you know what my brother did? *He put the cap back on the bottle!*"

The Soviets may have been a nuclear power but all they ever blew up was Chernobyl. I was in Poland when it happened. I said to a Pole, "I understand that because of the fallout we're supposed to avoid fresh vegetables."

He said, *"Fresh vegetables?"*

As ugly as Chernobyl was, it was nothing compared to commie couture. Older men wore Harry Truman suits but looking as if they'd been fitted to Harry and worn by Hervé Villechaize on *Fantasy Island*. Older women wore housedresses so ugly and so flowered that our grandmothers, even in their most muttering-to-themselves-in-the-kitchen mode, would have recoiled in horror. Young people tried to be hep. But it didn't work. One youthful Soviet minder, who'd been assigned to me as my translator, wore a pair of blue jeans in the most wrong possible blue and as un-jean-like in cut and as denim-less as a burka. On the back of these was a patch of fake leather, imitating the Levi's patch except three times too large, upon which was emblazoned "Dakota Jean" with *Dakota* misspelled in several places.

The Baby Boom was laughing at the communists. Finally, on November 9, 1989, the East German communists, being sensitive to ridicule the way Germans are, gave up on Marxist/Leninism, and the Berlin Wall came down.

For totalitarianism to work everybody has to keep a straight face. Dictators don't stand a chance with the Baby Boom—the Hitler snot comb mustache, the Mussolini beanie, Mao lacking only a gold chain to be dressed like a fat swinger in a Nehru jacket, plus all those silly dictator arm gestures. Baby Boomers would be Photoshopping their cats. Notice how the leaders of today's China are careful to appear in public looking like they're headed to a funeral—probably their own. I'll bet "Chairman Meow" memes are all over Chinese microblogs. And not to bring Jimmy Buffett into this again, but did you ever notice how Stalin kind of looks like Jimmy when Buffett had hair and a mustache? If the Russians had posted videos of Stalin lip-syncing "Margaritaville," Uncle Joe would have had to go gulag his own bad self.

The Baby Boom is the generation of the mocking tongue. The pen may be mightier than the sword but not once you get people howling with laughter. A couple of spit takes and the ink runs, the sword rusts, and the Baby Boom triumphs.

It will take a while to turn the whole world into Baby Boomers. For one thing, due to declining birthrates, they won't be a boom like we were with the same weight of numbers on their side. On the other hand, aging populations in places such as Russia and China will let these babies speak in booming voices. And a lot of the world is still stuck in the Idiot Generation and hasn't progressed to Greatest let alone attained the glory of B.B. But Muammar Gaddafi's clothes, grooming, and arm gestures were so dictator-ridiculous that even the fool Lybians shot him.

Also, there's a little bit of the Baby Boom in everyone. I was in Lebanon in 1984 during the civil war, and I was stopped at a checkpoint manned—or I should say boyed—by fifteen- and sixteen-year-old members of the militant Islamic fundamentalist Hezbollah. They were waving their AK-47s around, digging the barrels into the dirt and scratching their ears with the muzzle sights. (Gun safety courses must go begging in Lebanon.) One of the young militants pointed his AK-47 at my face. (It's surprising how small the hole is in the end of an AK-47, considering what a big difference it could make in your social life.) He demanded my passport. When he saw that I was an American he subjected me to a twenty-minute tirade, at gunpoint, about America Satan Devil and how the United States had caused the Lebanese civil war, colonialism, imperialism, Zionism, and every other problem he could think of. Then he handed my passport back and said, "As soon as I get my green card I am going to dentist school in Dearborn, Michigan."

Militant Islamic fundamentalism probably had a tough time surviving the karaoke nights and Craigslist personals of the Detroit metropolitan area. I bet the teenager who pointed the gun at me is now a wealthy orthodontist living in Bloomfield Hills.

* * *

Noxious politics will disappear as all the world's political science classes happily degenerate into hour-long shouting matches the way Jim Fisk's Constitutional Law class did. It's hard to remain truly noxious when you like being obnoxious better.

Stupid notions of central planning, nationalization, and protectionist trade barriers will fall by the wayside when everyone is paying as little attention in Economics as I was.

And sooner or later the 1.29 billion people making $1.25 a day, the way we were, selling *Puddles* on the street in Baltimore, are going to figure out there's a better way. I just received an e-mail from Nigeria about a rather large amount of money needing to be transferred to an American bank and requiring only modest assistance on my part.

There will be no religious fanaticism. We're not a generation who listens to anybody, God included. In our defense, I doubt God minds us not bothering about Him. Very few of the people we've bothered—parents, college deans, the police, LBJ, the psychiatrist at my draft physical, supervisors, bosses, attractive types in bars—have minded when we quit bothering them. Religious fanatics must be pesky from a heavenly point of view. "Now what?" thundered the Lord.

We're more sports fanatics. Yahweh hikes the ball to Jesus. Does Jesus hand off to Muhammad for short yardage? Buddha and Krishna are covered midfield. Secular Humanism is wide open for a long pass but he seems to be chatting with a cheerleader.

There will be no suicide bombings. Baby Boomers aren't going to strap explosive vests around our middles; it would make us look fat.

There will be no genocide or ethnic cleansing. One thing about the coddling and cosseting and doting upon that goes into creating a generation of spoiled brats is that it leaves us with a sentimental streak. Killing a whole race or ethnicity would involve doing away with quaint old people who possess time-honored wisdom (even if they are crabby with the kids in the neighborhood) and those kids in the neighborhood, too, not to mention major babes and ripped dudes. Plus a wholesale, warehouse store–type of hatred like that is too downmarket for the Baby Boom. When it comes to hating people, we like brand names. Furthermore, consider the progress science has made. Nowadays genocide would require everyone to be subjected to DNA testing. All those cotton swabs, what a bother.

There may be some outbreaks of sixties behavior in unexpected places. Perhaps that's what the Arab Spring is. Doesn't look too groovy to me, but whatever turns you on. A Saudi Arabian sit-in would be interesting because I've never seen the Saudis do anything but sit around anyway.

World peace is probably too much to ask. But it will be hard to assemble those huge conscripted armies that used to fight wars. We'll all have a letter from our doctor about our deep-seated psychiatric problems and drug use.

The hippie doctor who wrote mine happened to be a good doctor despite a practice constrained by crab lice. I was having some kidney problem and he sent me to a hospital for tests. A decade later the problem recurred. I had more tests and an appointment with an elderly kidney specialist. Looking into my medical file he began to back his chair away from mine. "Your kidneys are all right," he said. "But . . . do you need help?"

I had no idea what he was talking about, for a moment. Then I said, "Did the doctor's letter I took to my draft physical wind up in my medical files?"

"Aha!" said the elderly kidney specialist. "I wrote a lot of draft physical letters. But I never wrote one *this* good!"

Besides, war is about power. Baby Boomers are not power hungry. Power comes with that kicker, responsibility. We're greedy for love, happiness, experience, sensation, thrills, praise, fame, adulation, inner peace, and, as it turns out, money. Health and fitness too. But we're not greedy for power. Observe the Baby Boomers who have climbed to its ascendency in Washington. The best and the brightest? They're over at Goldman Sachs.

When we really are the world the place will be chaos. A universal Baby Boom will be running around everywhere doing anything they want at all hours of the day and night with nobody left to clean up. It may be a bad world.

But it will be a worse world for the Leaders of Men, looking around for their followers and wondering why everyone is following Keith Richards. It will be a terrible world for Authority. The Baby Boom will not countenance it. We turn our face from Authority. Indeed we turn our ass toward it. We moon Dominion.

Woe to you who have oppressed mankind with your theologies and your ideologies, your bigotries, doctrines, dogmas, and no sex until after we're married. Desolation awaits you who have foisted war upon us, subjugated us, yoked us, fettered us, and told us we can't get down and boogie.

You shall be as the ants beneath our magnifying glasses, the sand wasps affronted with our tennis rackets, the frogs ingesting our fireworks, the cats between our garages, the birdbaths, garden gnomes, and glass gazing balls at the mercy of our Wham-O slingshots. Flaming bags of dog poop shall be set upon your front porches.

Think how we made a misery of the lives of our parents. If we can do that to our dearest beloved, think what we can do to you. For that matter think what we did to ourselves. You shall spend eternity at a "Model UN." You shall listen forever to lectures of Margaret Mead. You shall sit upon a staircase inside a giant evil eel for all time. And if you go upstairs you'll be chewed by giant eel teeth. And if you go downstairs you'll be eel shit.

We are an obdurate generation. Our whim is iron. What we will to do is done. You, eel shit members of the Chinese politburo, have had a taste of this in Tiananmen Square. You remember the fellow blocking the tank. But do you remember the crucial detail? He was carrying shopping bags. Not only were you violating his human liberties, you were interfering with his shopping, a Baby Boom birthright. One man is a majority with shopping on his side.

You loathsome communists got away with it in Tiananmen Square. But for how long? The vengeance of the Baby Boom can be delayed but not denied. There will come a day, Xi Jinping, when the power and the dignity of your office shall be rendered so low that you shall appear as guest host on *Saturday Night Live*.

And what about you, detestable Taliban and Al-Qaeda and Osama wannabes cowering in your Waziristan, Kandahar, Yemen, and Mali hidey-holes? You who are pursued by those things perfectly christened with the name Baby Boomers have so often been called, drones. And when it comes to Baby Boom lethal technology, drones are nothing. How will things be with you when your bevy of wives discover vibrators?

And you, contemptible Putin? How long will your shirt-less self escape the LGBT float in the Greenwich Village Halloween Parade?

And all the rest of you tyrannical, despotic, overbearing squares and wet smacks with your two-bit autocracies in the butt ends of the world? You shall gather in finished basements while your revered elders stand at the top of the basement stairs yelling, "I think something's on fire down there!" Your offices shall be liberated by Balto-Cong. You shall spend your treasure on cocaine and rehab. Your junk bonds shall default. You shall form overage garage bands and try to play "Margaritaville." Your third spouse shall acquire an American Express Black Card with a credit limit higher than the U.S. national debt. Your daughters shall wear nose rings. Your sons shall have pagan symbols indelibly marked upon their necks. (Unless you belong to one of those cultures where daughters wear nose rings and sons have pagan symbols indelibly marked upon their necks, in which case they shall not.) You shall be perplexed by the Internet. You shall grow old and addled enough to vote for Ron Paul in a presidential primary.

There is no escape from happiness, attention, affection, freedom, irresponsibility, money, peace, opportunity, and finding out that everything you were ever told is bullshit. Behold the Baby Boom, ye mighty, and despair.

Much did I rage when young,
Being by the world oppressed,
But now with flattering tongue
It speeds the parting guest.
— William Butler Yeats,
"Youth and Age"

Acknowledgments

We may glean wisdom from the worst fools, or what are writers for? A greater fool than even the present writer was communist dupe Maxim Gorky. In a speech to the Congress of Soviet Writers in 1934, Gorky said, "The basic hero of our books should be labor; that is, man organized by the process of labor."

If Gorki's advice were followed, literature would be the plucking and gutting production line in a Perdue chicken processing plant, and readers would be up to their bifocals in feathers and gizzards. But when it comes to writing "Acknowledgments," Gorky may have been on to something. The basic hero of this book is man organized by the process of labor in the form of Grove/Atlantic, Inc.

Morgan Entrekin is my friend, my editor, my publisher, and my Hercules. He goes forth daily to perform his labors. He snatches the Pulitzer Prize–winning golden apple authors of the Hesperides, catches the Erymanthian Boar of bad writing before it gets into print, braves the poisonous fumes of the nine-headed Hydra of book reviewing, captures the Cerberus hell-hound of the modern book buyer's attention span, and otherwise cleanses the Augean stables of the publishing industry. Count him among the immortals.

Associate publisher Judy Hottensen, publicity director Deb Seager, and publicist Scott Manning are saintly Melchior, Caspar, and Balthazar in the marketing of books. Never mind if this particular star they're following is an *ignis fatuus*. In all other cases their gold, frankincense, and myrrh are delivered to the correct address.

Art director Charles Rue Woods works always in the heroic scale, as the cover of this tome attests. I salute his intrepid industry as he perched upon the rickety scaffold of my scribbling to give a Sistine Chapel ceiling to the privy I have constructed.

Associate editor Peter Blackstock is the Chevalier de Bayard, the knight *sans peur et sans reproche* of editing. Without Peter, there would have been no chivalry in the grubby battle to produce a book.

Copyeditor Don Kennison played brave Galileo during the tortures of the Inquisition to which I subjected spelling, punctuation, and the English language in general. Often I forced him to renounce his accurate contention that Earth's prose style revolves around the sun of grammar and sense. But his courage never failed. He exited saying, "And yet it moves."

Managing editor Amy Vreeland and production director Sue Cole have—what is more valiant?— managed and produced. No Penelope beset by suitors coped better than they with waiting for the long overdue Odysseus, in the form of corrected proofs, to come slay that horde of unwelcome swains known as deadlines.

And let us give medals and erect monuments to sales assistant Becca Putman, digital manager Michael Dudding, and social media manager Jessica Monahan. I confess, due to my e-senility, that I don't know exactly what digital and social media managing are, so Michael and Jessica become my Unknown Soldiers, but here, as at Arlington, all the more honored for being so.

Lastly there are, among the paragons, eight muses rolled into one: my wife, Tina. She is Calliope, muse of epic poetry, for inspiration in attempting to make an epic of the Baby Boom's comedy, and Thalia, muse of comedy, for inspiration in attempting the reverse. She is Clio, muse of history, listening to my old stories over and over without letting her head explode. She is song's Euterpe, crooning when things went well, tragedy's Melpomene, comforting when things didn't, and love's Erato always. She is Polyhymnia for her hymns of praise and prayers of criticism. And she is Terpsichore in her dance of attendance upon the children and the household cares while I was locked in a room for sixteen hours a day writing or, as it is properly called, staring out the window doing nothing.

This leaves one muse, Urania, whose domain is astronomy. That would be my old hunting dog, Millie, who has spent the past year in an armchair in my office, staunch ally in staring out the window doing nothing.